ADVANCED COMPUTERS

PARALLEL AND BIOCHIP PROCESSORS

BY

NORMAN W. LORD
PAUL A. GIROGOSIAN
ROBERT P. OUELLETTE
ROBERT J. CLERMAN
PAUL N. CHEREMISINOFF

ANN ARBOR SCIENCE
THE BUTTERWORTH GROUP

230 Collingwood, P.O. Box 1425, Ann Arbor, Michigan 48106

Library of Congress Catalog Card Number 82-46062
ISBN 0-250-40626-8

Manufactured in the United States of America

Butterworths, Ltd., Borough Green
Sevenoaks, Kent TN15 8PH, England

PREFACE

The science of computers with its many languages and complex operational procedures is a rapidly advancing technology. The field has so developed that computers can be programmed for many different methods of solution, and applications and uses are growing exponentially.

This book presents a detailed study on advanced computers. It is organized in two sections covering vector/parallel computers (evaluation, uses and case histories in practice) and a state-of-the-art survey of biochip technology.

Section 1 deals with a new generation of very high-speed computers now available. This computer generation contains vector and parallel processors capable of high program-execution speeds by simultaneous processing of instructions on multiple sets of input data. The various applications for such high-speed computational capabilities are described with the vector/parallel processors that are commercially available to meet their requirements. The background and computational advantages of vector/parallel processing concepts, as well as a survey of the available equipment with attendant advantages and experiences, are given.

This book describes the differences in computational capacities offered by the new systems in the context of applications. Comparisons of commercial systems are made. Technical background (describing the relevant features of vector/parallel processors), results of field surveys of equipment, and prospective hardware and software developments are discussed.

Section 2 presents the state-of-the-art of biochip technology and bioelectronics. Included are: biological processes and materials in device fabrication with recent developments in the use of protein and other biological materials, molecular circuitry (conceptual designs for three-dimensional devices that mimic biochemical electron transport), and biosensors (field effect transistors that sense and respond to electrical potential created by biochemical reactions). The future outlook for bioelectronics is discussed along with R&D strategies for microelectronics.

Grateful acknowledgement for support of these studies and the resultant book is made to Euratrom, of the Commission of European Communities, for the work on vector/parallel processors, and to Electricité de France, the French national electric utility, for the survey work in bioelectronics.

Norman W. Lord
Paul A. Giragosian
Robert P. Ouellette
Robert J. Clerman
Paul N. Cheremisinoff

Norman W. Lord is a broad-spectrum physicist with the MITRE Corporation. He has consulted extensively for government and industries on a wide variety of problems in operations and estimating technological trends. He received his BEE from Brooklyn Polytechnic Institute and his MA and PhD in Physics from Columbia University. Dr. Lord has been a research physicist at Johns Hopkins University Applied Physics Laboratory, Hudson Laboratories of Columbia University and Travelers Research Center (Hartford, Connecticut). He is co-author of a number of books published by Ann Arbor Science, including: *Coal-Oil Mixture Technology*, *Heat-Pump Technology*, and *Advances In Electric Heat Treatment of Metals*.

Paul A. Giragosian is currently a member of the technical staff at the MITRE Corporation, where he is concerned with state-of-the-art technologies in the areas of computer architecture, telecommunications and systems engineering. His education includes studies at the State University of New York at Binghamton, where he received a BA in Physics and MS in Computer Science. Mr. Giragosian has a broad and varied background in the field of computer applications. He has conducted original research in image evaluation and the measurement of information capacity of photographic materials through the use of artificial intelligence techniques. Other areas of research include heuristic programming and operations research applications. He is a member of IEEE Computer Society, ACM and SPSE, and has acted as organizer of numerous seminars devoted to the state-of-the-art computer architectures.

Robert P. Ouellette is Technical Director for the Environmental Division of the MITRE Corporation. Dr. Ouellette has been associated with MITRE in varying capacities since 1969. Earlier, he was with TRW Systems, Hazelton Labs Inc. and Massachusetts General Hospital. A graduate of the University of Montreal, he received his PhD from the University of Ottawa. He is a member of the American Statistical Association, Biometrics Society, Atomic Industrial Forum and the National Science Foundation Technical Advisory Panel on Hazardous Substances. Dr. Ouellette has published numerous technical papers and books on energy and the environment and is co-editor/co-author of the Electrotechnology series published by Ann Arbor Science.

Robert J. Clerman is a group leader in the Environmental Division of the MITRE Corporation. He received his BS in Biology from the State University of New York at Fredonia and his MS in Environmental Sciences from the University of Virginia. His research interests and publications have covered a wide range of environmental and technical issues. Projects have included development of a tiered testing system for new chemicals evaluation, design of a residuals monitoring program (both for the Federal Republic of Germany), and evaluation of organic pollutants in water (for the Department of Energy and the National Cancer Institute). Currently, he is managing studies of industrial applications of biotechnology.

Paul N. Cheremisinoff is Associate Professor at New Jersey Institute of Technology. He is a consulting engineer and has been consultant on environmental/energy/resources projects for the MITRE Corporation. He has more than 30 years of practical design, research/development and engineering experience in a wide range of industries including pollution control, waste treatment, chemical and process industries. He is author/editor of many Ann Arbor Science publications, including: *Pollution Engineering Practice Handbook*, *Carbon Adsorption Handbook* and *Environmental Impact Data Book*.

CONTENTS

Section 1
Vector/Parallel Processing Computers

Section 2
Biochip Technology

FIGURES AND TABLES

FIGURES

TABLES

SECTION 1

VECTOR/PARALLEL PROCESSING COMPUTERS

CHAPTER 1

INTRODUCTION

During the past few years, a new generation of very-high-speed general-purpose computers has become available on the open market. The leading edge of this computer generation is comprised of vector and parallel processors that attain their high program-execution speeds by concurrent processing of instructions on multiple sets of input data.

Application categories of interest include:

- nuclear reactor operation;
- nuclear reactor safety;
- waste disposal;
- nuclear fuel cycle;
- safeguards;
- fusion;
- new and renewable energy resources;
- environmental study of uptake (migration and toxicity) of pollutants;
- real-time remote data processing via satellite;
- image processing; and
- remote sensing from space.

To meet high-speed computational needs in such areas, three general-purpose vector/parallel processors are marketed commercially in the United States:

1. CRAY-1S,
2. Control Data Corporation CYBER 200 Model 205, and
3. Denelcor Heterogeneous Element Processor.

Until very recently, there were two other vector/parallel processors: the Burroughs Scientific Processors, derived from the ILLIAC IV, and the ICL Distributed Array Processor. However, Burroughs and ICL have been reported to be withdrawing from this market in the United States; there are no current or prospective U.S. users.

Another very-high-speed general-purpose computer of more conventional architecture is the Amdahl 580, which is just beginning to be marketed. It appeals to some users as a conventional alternative.

There are also special-purpose vector/parallel processors:

1. Goodyear Aerospace Massively Parallel Processor;
2. Floating Point Systems AP-120B, AP190L, FPS-164 Array Processors;
3. Data General Eclipse AP130 Array Processor;
4. IBM 3838 Array Processor; and
5. Control Data Corporation Advanced Flexible Processor.

However, these processors are designed primarily to provide supplemental vector processing capability to existing minicomputer or large mainframe configurations. These devices will not be considered further, as they do not provide memory capacity, throughput rate or computational speeds adequate for reasonable execution times in the application areas discussed in this book.

The computational advantages of vector/parallel processing concepts are realized when a sequence of independent similar arithmetic operations are performed. As long as the results of any operation are not required for any other operation in the sequence, high computational speed may be achieved, in proper execution of the algorithm, if the operations are performed simultaneously. Moreover, if the input data for these operations are similar and in contiguous locations, the data can be fetched and supplied to the arithmetic unit at great speed through special "vector" registers. The term "vector" is taken from consideration of data elements as components of a vector. A background discussion of the vector/parallel processing concept, with some comparison among the chief features of the three commercial systems of concern, is provided in Chapter 5. There is a wide range of speed improvement offered by the new systems, depending on the combination of particular systems and particular applications. It is generally a factor between 2 and 10. This book describes the main differences in the computational capacities offered by the new systems in the context of applications within the cited areas of special interest.

The technical approach of the study was carried out as follows:

1. Background literature, much of it supplied by manufacturers' representatives and user organizations, was used to establish the main relevant features of the new capacity and the main lines of application for which the systems were expected to provide the biggest advantage.
2. Industrial representatives were contacted to explain the distinguishing features of

their systems, including machine architecture, circuit logic, large-scale circuit arrangement, operating features and software. Additionally, their expectations of future developments in hardware and software were solicited.

3. Computer centers that were current or prospective users of the advanced systems were first contacted for preliminary information about their experience or expectation, and then later for a much more detailed interview, following a standard survey format (see the appendix). Included in the survey were discussions of future developments that may be inspired by the upward trend in computational requirements.
4. The study was organized into four tasks. First, a technical background describing the relevant features of vector/parallel processors was prepared. Second, the results of the survey were organized for a report in detail for each user and in collective summary for each major topic of the survey. Then, brief discussions of prospective hardware developments and prospective software developments were prepared.

CHAPTER 2

USER EVALUATION OF VECTOR/PARALLEL PROCESSING COMPUTERS

This summary of the experience and assessment of the most prominent current and prospective users of vector and parallel processors is based on a detailed survey recounted in detail in Chapter 6. Each organization has decided that, for its particular assortment of applications and staff resources, the potential computing speed improvements of the computer selected will largely be realized and will offset the costs and extra work of converting to a vector or parallel processor system.

Table 2-1 identifies user organizations, their major application areas and their selected processors: CRAY-1, CRAY-1S, Control Data Corporation (CDC) CYBER 205 or Denelcor (Heterogeneous Element Processor (HEP). As a counter-example, one organization (the U.S. Air Force North American Defense Command) that is considering the more conventional Amdahl 580 is also included. The application area of modeling atmosphere and ocean dynamics has been added to include a discussion of the most pertinent cases when the CDC CYBER 205 was selected over the CRAY. According to our best information at present, no organizations are concerned with image processing using any vector/parallel processing computer.

From Table 2-1 it is apparent that CRAY-1 and CRAY-1S processors have been selected by a majority of the organizations engaged in the cited areas of primary interest. However, out of seven nuclear energy laboratories, only two (Knolls and Bettis) selected the CDC CYBER 205, along with the National Aeronautics and Space Administration (NASA) Goddard Laboratory for Atmospheric Sciences (GLAS). In the area of atmospheric processes and weather modeling, the CDC CYBER 205 was also selected by the Geophysical Fluid Dynamics Laboratory (GFDL) of the National Oceanic and Atmospheric Administration (NOAA). Both

Table 2-1. Application and User/Processor Distributions

Processor Type	User	Application Area[a]											
		1	2	3	4	5	6	7	8	9	10	11	12
CRAY-1S	LLL	X	X	X	X		X	X	X	X			
	NMFECC						X		X				
	LANL	X	X	X	X	X	X	X					
	Sandia—Livermore		X					X	X				
	Sandia—Albuquerque		X	X			X	X					
	Boeing Computing Service								X				
	United Computing Service								X				
	Westinghouse Nuclear Energy Center	X	X	X	X								
CDC CYBER 205	U.S. Air Force Weapons Laboratory										X		
CDC CYBER 205	GLAS									X	X		X
	GFDL												X
	Knolls Atomic Power Laboratory	X	X	X	X								
	Bettis Atomic Power Laboratory	X	X	X	X								
Denelcor HEP	Cornell University						X						
	Brookhaven National Laboratory	X	X	X	X	X	X						
Amdahl 5860	U.S. Air Force North American Defense Command										X		

[a]Key: 1 = nuclear reactor operation; 2 = nuclear reactor safety; 3 = waste disposal; 4 = nuclear fuel cycle; 5 = safeguards; 6 = fusion; 7 = new and renewable energy sources; 8 = environmental study of pollutant uptake; 9 = real-time remote data processing via satellite; 10 = remote sensing from space; 11 = image processing; 12 = atmosphere and ocean dynamics.

GLAS and GFDL are primarily interested in applying their most powerful computers to problems of weather and atmospheric processes. Although, for each organization, several special areas of interest are indicated in Table 2-1, some areas are not expected to require or be able to profitably use vector/parallel processing computers. In particular, the areas of waste disposal, real-time remote data processing via satellite and remote sensing from space, although they were part of their activities, were generally not expected by staff members of the user organizations to pose any special demands for high-speed computer capability.

Although there is an apparent preference among the organizations for the CRAY-1S computer, one must also recognize the historical background for this. Most of the user organizations are primarily concerned with developing nuclear energy technology. Some of them participated in the earliest days of this work under direction of the U.S. Atomic Energy Commission (AEC). Digital computers were developed about the same time as the AEC was formed in the late 1940s. The AEC computers were first used in nuclear weapons development to analyze multidimensional fluid dynamics effects. Their potential use for nuclear reactor design and high-energy physics problems was quickly realized. Neutron diffusion problems in reactors were similar to those of weapons, and the computers were very useful in processing large amounts of data from bubble-chamber, spark-chamber and other experiments associated with high-energy particle accelerators. A long-standing and continuing tradition of using the most advanced computers available was firmly established in the laboratories engaged in nuclear energy development. When the early CRAY models were first offered commercially in 1976, they were immediately adopted in laboratories supported by the U.S. Energy Research and Development Administration (ERDA), which succeeded the AEC in nuclear technology development. It was another four years before the CDC CYBER 205 became available as a possible alternative. By then, a number of the laboratories had become comfortably experienced in using the CRAY system and whatever marginal improvement may be offered by a very different computer, such as the CDC CYBER 205, could not outweigh the troubles of system conversion.

The first section below describes some highlights of the computation activities commonly engaged in by the user organizations within the application areas of special interest for high-speed computing. Some of the typical computation requirements are described for each user organization contacted for a detailed survey. The last section discusses some of the major concerns underlying the selection of vector or parallel processors, how the systems have been evaluated, advantages and problems of the different systems, and some of the most pertinent details of the organizations' experience in carrying out the system conversion.

APPLICATION AREAS REQUIRING ADVANCED COMPUTING CAPABILITY

The utility of vector or parallel processing systems, as discussed in Chapter 5, depends critically on the nature of the computations being performed. As pointed out above, for some application areas of special interest there is no particular reason to use a high-capacity computer. Whatever simulation studies may be carried out for these areas are simple in their computing requirements, and computing equipment may be used mostly for input/output (I/O) operations. The special advantage of the advanced computers is centered strictly on the capability to carry out arithmetical operations at high speed; to use this advantage, the sequence of required elementary computations must fit the vector/parallel architecture of operation and data access arrangements. If the underlying algorithm or its expression in a computer program cannot be modified to include long sequences of independent operations on rapidly accessed data, the program will be executed mainly in the conventional manner (a sequence of single instruction executions). This may still take advantage of speed improvements due to electronic design of the CRAY and CDC CYBER computers, which are both somewhat faster in their scalar operation modes than are conventional systems. However, the full advantage of vector processing can only be realized for computations that can be formulated appropriately.

Presently, selection of a vector or parallel processor is based primarily on a judgment that eventually the major portion of their computational requirement could be reformulated to take advantage of the capability to process a number of instructions in a program simultaneously. Since the work of program reformulation is still in progress, it is not always possible to cite exactly how appropriate a specific computation may be for the vector or parallel processor. The problems described in the following sections, however, illustrate the major requirements that are expected to be met by the vector/parallel processors.

Nuclear Reactor Operation

Large, detailed systems codes for nuclear reactors are usually devised for design and safety analysis. They are required to predict the gross operational parameters for a power plant and the parameters associated with the thermohydraulic state of the primary coolant system, such as the fuel rod centerline temperature, the peak cladding temperature, heat flux from fuel rods to water and, possibly, fission products generated. (Codes emphasizing the abnormal conditions associated with various accidents are discussed in the section on reactor safety.) Codes designed to simulate normal reactor operation can usually be broken down to those for separate processes, such as core neutron dynamics, fuel behavior or coolant system components (e.g., primary loop or steam generator). For example, the COBRA and MEKIN codes analyze the core fission heat generation [Bowring et al. 1975; Wheeler et al. 1976].

Such codes face a fundamental difficulty in using vector/parallel processing computers. Calculating the transport and energy changes of fission neutrons inside the fuel rod is most accurately done by direct simulation of individual neutron histories using the Monte Carlo technique. The neutron moves stochastically in a Markoff process between states, with each transition governed by a set of probability functions that depend only on the current state. The various probability distributions are then sampled randomly to determine the sequence of states. The code name "Monte Carlo" was given to this method at the Los Alamos National Laboratory (LANL) during World War II. Use of ENIAC was anticipated for the first computer application, and the method has always required large amounts of computer time for the sample sizes and accuracies desired.

Unfortunately, efforts to vectorize Monte Carlo codes have not been very successful. There is an apparent parallelism in the problem that cannot be carried through. Tracking the progress of each particle is independent of all other particle histories. However, the sequence of computations performed on each history vary depending on the random sampling of the probability distributions. It is very difficult to develop and process queues of similar computations. Jordan [1979] has been attempting to solve this problem using artificial production codes and testing them against multiprocessor arrangements.

Nuclear Reactor Safety

Analysis of accident consequences would be impractical by performing experiments on operating reactors. Instead, reactor behavior during hypothetical accidents, testing the adequacy of emergency safety systems, is usually evaluated by computer simulations of operation under the abnormal conditions of the accident [Buzbee et al. 1980]. Such programs have strained the capabilities of computers such as the CDC 7600, taking up to 20 hours. The U.S. Nuclear Regulatory Commission (NRC) wanted to analyze the Three Mile Island accident in a program of numerical simulations with many different sets of assumptions. However, the computations would have occupied 15% of the scientific computers in the United States, and the program was reduced. Considerable information was gained by computer analysis.

One of the most important general assessments of nuclear reactor safety has been the study undertaken by NRC [1975]. A central element in the methodology of this study is a fault tree analysis. This technique provides a systematic method of relating system failure probabilities to basic component failure and event probabilities. This methodology is still being refined and exercised at nuclear energy laboratories to take into account new findings.

Fault tree analysis produces a logic diagram showing how component failure modes and other fault events produce system failure as a consequence of AND and OR combinatorial logic. The fault tree is a binary model of the fault modes of a system, which converts to a probabilistic model of the system. In this model, failure probabilities can be assigned to individual elements and combined to obtain system failure probabilities. Failure data for individual fault tree events include component failure rates, fault duration times, unavailabilities of subsystems and components due to test or maintenance, probability of human errors, and other miscellaneous fault probabilities. Error factors that express variabilities in the data are applied to individual failure rate values so that probability range for system failure can be determined through Monte Carlo calculations. By almost all considerations of implementing the algorithms that carry out a fault tree analysis, it would be very difficult to cast them in a vectorized form. At best, the analysis would benefit from the scalar calculation improvement in systems such as the CRAY-1S.

Nuclear energy laboratories also collaborate with NRC to develop computer codes simulating the behavior of core fuel elements and steam-generating equipment. In particular, the codes are important in the investigation of the likelihood and scale of transients in reactor behavior and thermohydraulic consequences of equipment breakdown, such as loss of coolant [Wulff 1981]. Computer program runs are used to investigate system response, control room instrumentation and operator action in plant transients that lead to degraded core conditions. Modeling results assist in planning of experiments and analysis of experimental results. Such codes are expected to begin from a realistic steady-state condition to predict the thermohydraulic transients induced by four generic classes of sudden abnormal conditions:

1. Reactivity insertion, setback or scram requires modeling prompt and delayed neutron transport processes, decay heat generation, boron transport, control rod actions, and nonequilibrium boiling that forms voids in the coolant subject to collapse and that feed back their own influence reactivity.
2. Losses of collant inventory, either by pipe break, instrument line break or by valve failure call, for example, for modeling nonequilibrium boiling, phase separation and a variety of coolant system malfunctions.
3. Loss of heat sink, either a steam generator in PWR or a turbine trip in boiling water reactors (BWR) may be accompanied by reactor scram and lead at least temporarily to core overheating.
4. Startup, shutdown or failure of primary coolant or recirculation pumps requires centrifugal pump models covering operation as pumps or turbines, in normal and reverse flows, and combinations of vapor and liquid phases.

Two of the most important recent lines of code development for such cases have been the RELAP series, presently at RELAP 5 [Wagner et al. 1981], developed at the Idaho National Engineering Laboratory, and

TRAC [Vigil and Knight 1981], developed at LANL. Both of these developments emphasize the use of a two-fluid approach for modeling the liquid and vapor phases. RELAP 5 has been implemented on a CDC CYBER 170 and TRAC has been implemented on a CDC 7600.

The series of codes known as SAS, used to analyze hypothetical accidents in liquid-metal fast-breeder reactors (LMFBR), has been modified, in its current production version, SAS 3D, to run on the CRAY-1 [Dunn and Kyser 1979]. In various versions, run time improvements have been achieved over the IBM 370-195 of 2.5–7X.

To analyze the structural safety of nuclear reactors, computer codes have been developed to predict the performance of nuclear structures under extreme loading conditions, such as earthquakes, which are difficult to simulate physically. The standards used by NRC have evolved from historical practice in the design of pressure vessels, concrete buildings and steel structures. They have been modified for nuclear plant structures to reflect more stringent requirements for safety margins against failure, as well as the essential differences between conventional structures and nuclear plant configurations. Computer codes for simulation of structural behavior are, therefore, essential in trying to predict the consequences of this twofold extrapolation from prior structural experience. One of the most promising refinements, developed by Hallquist [1981], is the DYNA3D program for modeling and graphic display of material deformation. It is a Lagrangian, finite-deformation, finite-element computer program that solves the momentum equations and the conservation equations of mass and energy. Three-dimensional studies are made of the interaction of nuclear reactor structures with the surrounding soil. An earthquake analysis using DYNA3D is shown in Figure 2-1.

Nuclear Fuel Cycle

Besides reactor operation, most other stages of the nuclear fuel cycle, such as mining, fuel element fabrication and reprocessing, require only casual use of computers in any analytic capacity. However, for some of the advanced isotope enrichment techniques under development, there is a requirement for very exacting description of the physical state transitions taking place. For example, in the use of lasers for isotope separation, the effects on the uranium atom are central, e.g., intense fields, multiphoton phenomena, coherence and saturation. The basic approach to achieving some understanding of the theoretical problems uses phenomenological models that are in part theoretical but normalized according to known experimental results. On the uranium atom, Hartree-

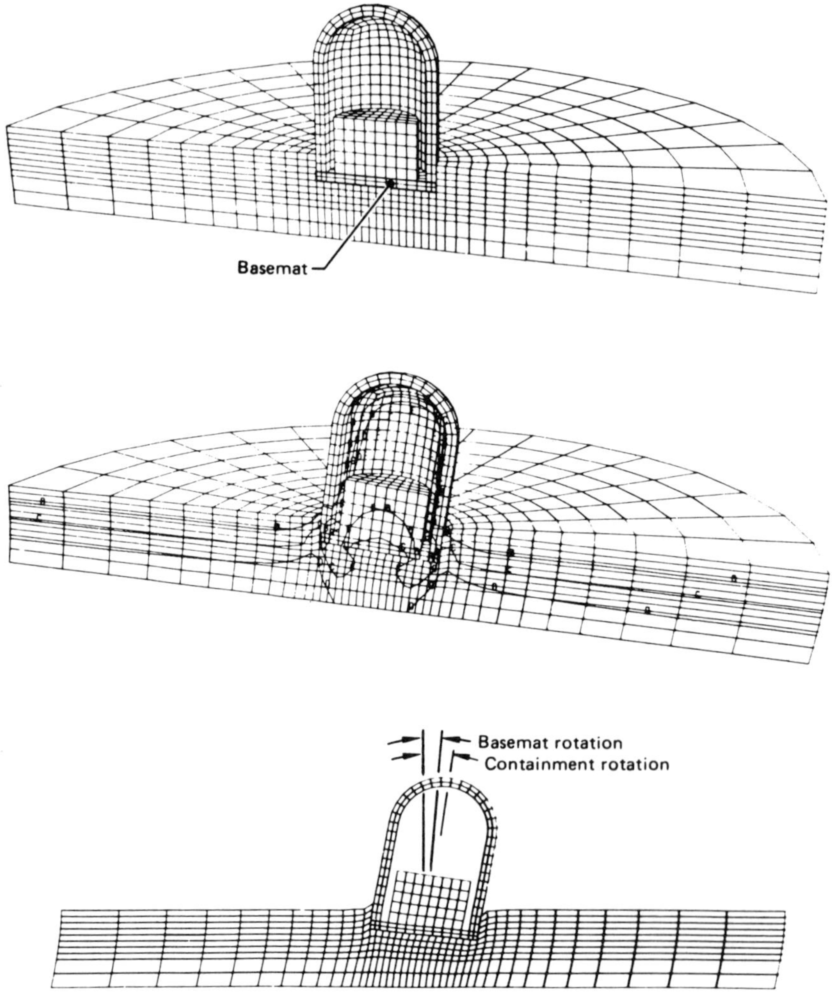

Figure 2-1. Earthquake analysis of a nuclear reactor using DYNA3D and detailed soil model. Top: finite element mesh of starting condition. Center: contours of shear stress. Bottom: basemat and reactor containment structure after earthquake [Hallquist 1981].

Fock calculations of electronic wave functions were used to determine starting parameters of a nonlinear optimization process to shape the functions to be consistent with experimentally observed atomic spectra.

The underlying research can be divided into a number of areas, including atomic and molecular structure, dynamics, electron scattering and photoionization, kinetics, and photon physics. To illuminate one example in terms of the computational load, consider atomic and molecular structure studies for prediction, calculation and interpretation of energy levels and complex potential energy surfaces. In some cases, large matrices (10^6 to 10^7 matrix elements) must be formed, manipulated and diagonalized. Certain approaches, such as sparse matrix techniques, can be used where applicable, to reduce the number of computer operations, but there always remains a large requirement of exactly the kind for which vector/parallel processors were designed. The advanced isotope enrichment programs under U.S. Department of Energy (DOE) sponsorship are still at an early stage and there are as yet no specific code development results available to report.

Safeguards

A major goal of safeguards systems is to protect material containing significant quantities of fissile isotopes from any form of theft or sabotage. Nuclear fuel cycle facilities handling such material include (1) physical security systems that control access; and (2) material accounting systems intended to monitor closely the amounts of such material received, generated and stored in the facility.

NRC and DOE set policy to determine the level of protection that facilities handling such material must maintain. These agencies also inspect facilities to ensure that their safeguards meet the established requirements. At the Lawrence Livermore Laboratory (LLL), a method of analysis called Aggregated System Model (ASM) has been developed [Al-Ayat 1981] to provide some quantitative judgments that can establish and ensure compliance with NRC/DOE safeguards requirements. The ASM divides the problem of safeguards analysis into four stages:

1. threat representation,
2. scenario evaluation,
3. performance aggregation, and
4. consequence assessment.

A block diagram very roughly illustrating the operation of the model is shown in Figure 2-2.

In the first stage, threats are represented by scenarios of theft or sabotage, each scenario characterized by a hypothetical adversary and strategy. Important features of the adversary are level of authority, access to fissile material and a presumed goal, such as the theft of a specific quantity of material. Strategies are characterized by the quantity and form of the material sought, collusive associations, diversion path,

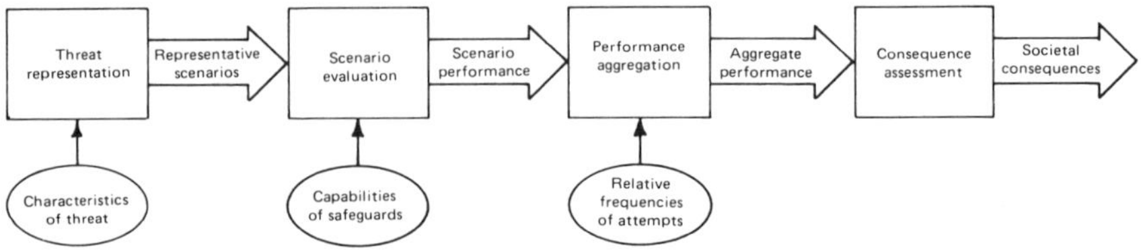

Figure 2-2. Aggregated systems model analysis of safeguards.

timing, tampering with records or monitoring instruments, and frequency of attempts. In the second stage, the scenarios are used to evaluate the performance of the safeguards systems. The measures of performance are the probabilities of detecting the attempt and preventing loss of material, and the expected time to detection from start of attempt. This yields a set of performance statistics, for each scenario, that summarizes the strengths and weaknesses of the safeguards. Scenarios against which safeguards are weak identify vulnerable points of the system. In the third stage of the analysis, an overall performance level for the system is judged by aggregating results over all expected combinations of adversary and preferred strategy. It is assumed that each adversary will select the strategy with the greatest chance of success. Relative likelihoods are assigned to each combination of adversary and preferred strategy. These are then used to estimate the weighted-average performance of the system of safeguards.

At this level of the analysis, the performance of a specified safeguard system has been quantified so that it can be determined whether it meets specified standards. One can also evaluate how possible modifications to the system would affect overall performance. Through comparisons, one can then identify alternatives that, by the measure of improvement in overall performance, are most cost-effective. To go beyond this, one must determine the appropriate level of safeguard standards and decide to what extent the improvement in performance warrants the cost. The fourth and most difficult stage of consequence assessment can then be used. The uncertainties of consequences and the tradeoffs among them are incorporated directly and explicitly into the program. Probability trees are used to represent the wide range of potential undesirable uses of fissile material. The analysis is useful in exploring wide ranges of value judgments on crucial variables of the safeguards so as to judge what level of protection costs for additional safeguards outweighs the benefit of associated reduction in public risk.

Several versions of the ASM have been implemented as computer programs for a number of applications. One focused on current attempts by insiders to steal fissile material to determine costs and benefits of implementing proposed new NRC regulations. The specific safeguard measures identified for improved performance depended markedly on the scenarios. For example, in some cases earlier theft detection was recommended, but in others it was better to reduce the likelihood of a successful theft.

Fusion

Computer applications relevant to thermonuclear fusion processes are different for the two main avenues of fusion device development: magnetic and inertial confinement of dense plasmas.

In magnetic fusion experiments, large numerical models are usually necessary to describe adequately the complicated physical phenomena in the plasma. Of the various kinds of numerical models for describing plasma behavior, time-dependent magnetohydrodynamic (MHD) codes, normal mode MHD calculations and particle codes are among the largest and longest-running codes in a network served by the LLL National Magnetic Fusion Energy Computer Center (NMFECC). The most general MHD problem requires the solution of eight simultaneous nonlinear partial differential equations. Three-dimensional calculations have been difficult to do on machines such as the CDC 7600. One of these was a numerical simulation of the SCYLAC experiment using a three-dimensional nonlinear MHD code [Barnes and Brackbill 1977]. It is now possible to perform these calculations much faster and with better resolution using the CRAY-1 system at NMFECC. In the CRAY-1 acceptance test, a LLL particle code was used. It is known as a 2.5-dimensional code because it assumes that quantities vary only in the radial and axial directions (cylindrical symmetry), but that particles may have velocities in all three coordinate directions [Killeen 1978].

The program has been used to investigate possible field-reversed configurations in some of the mirror fusion reactors and the Mirror Fusion Test Facility [Byers 1977]. In the current mirror fusion development at LLL, the plasma is confined inside a solenoid with end-leakage prevented by baseball or yin-yang coil arrangements for which field strength increases from the centerpoint in all directions [Carlson 1978]. Figure 2-3 shows the experimental arrangement with the main computations required to understand the operation of the device in terms of the available diagnostic instrumentation [Simonen 1981].

In the toroidal Tokamak device, the magnetic field lines confining the plasma are given a helical twist by a poloidal magnetic field generated

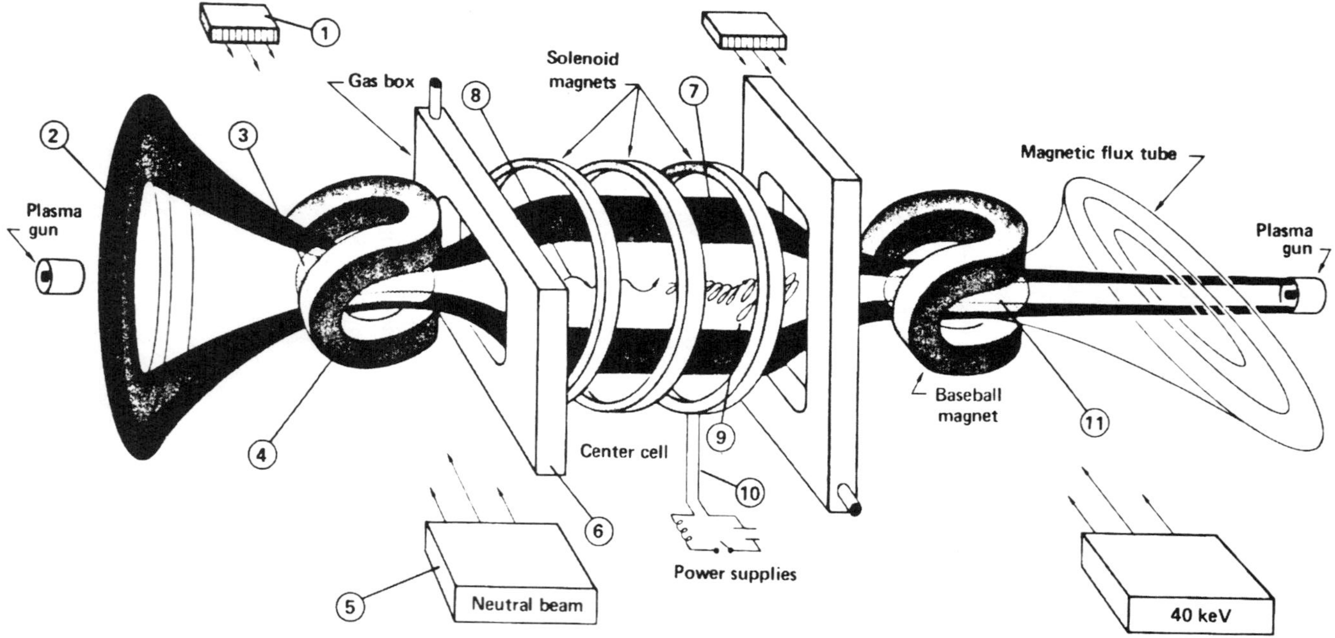

Figure 2-3. Tandem mirror fusion computations. 1 = design of accelerators, neutralizers and ion sources for neutral beams; 2 = end losses, secondary electron emission, $T_e(Z)$; 3 = high β, particle and MHD equilibria; 4 = baseball and other coil design stresses and fields; 5 = neutral beam penetration, heating and buildup; 6 = radial penetration of cold neutral gas; 7 = neoclassical radial transport, based on banana orbits; 8 = cyclotron RF instability simulation; 9 = stochastic heating of low-energy ion by RF in end plug; 10 = circuit and power supply design; 11 = self-consistent quasilinear diffusion and Fokker-Planck term [DOE 1979].

mainly by the current of the plasma circulating around the torus. The plasma is subject to instabilities, which can disrupt the confinement. Computer analysis of the MHD modes assists in studying the nature of the instabilities and how to suppress them. One approach uses the Lagrangian associated with linearized perturbations to formulate an eigenvalue problem. At the Princeton Plasma Physics laboratory, using the NMFECC CRAY network, one of the major codes of this category, the Princeton Equilibrium, Stability, and Transport (PEST) code, has been vectorized [Manikam 1979]. The result has been significant improvement in run times of various parts of the code with the capability to use finer spatial meshes for the reference frame due to increased local memory available from the CRAY. Depending on which function the code is carrying out, run time improvement varies from four- to ninefold. Another approach in studying instabilities has been applied to nonlinear growth of resistive heating MHD modes as precursors of major disruption [Hicks and Carreras 1979], also using the NMFECC network. Their code was formulated in FORTRAN shortly before the CRAY-1 was available, but in a style designed to facilitate vectorizing by the CRAY FORTRAN compiler. Execution times were about 25% as long on the CRAY-1 as on the CDC 7600.

In both mirror and Tokamak magnetic confinement, the plasma is subject to perturbations that give rise to non-Maxwellian energy distributions. The governing kinetic equation for each plasma species is the Boltzmann equation with a Fokker-Planck term representing the change in the distribution function due to Coulomb collisions. For a two-dimensional case, McCoy et al. [1979] developed a vectorized package by carefully arranging the structure of extensive nested loops used in the program. Their timing tests show that the vectorized program on the CRAY-1 runs faster by up to 12-fold over an optimized program run on the CDC 7600. It also runs faster by 3.65X over a nonvectorized program on the CRAY-1.

Fusion of inertially confined plasmas is possible by rapid laser heating of small target pellets with resultant implosions and the required high plasma densities reached at the center of the pellet. Design of the configuration of lasers and the pellets requires extensive computer analysis to understand the behavior of the targets. Current programs for designing targets use up to 20 hours per run [Buzbee et al. 1980]. In addition, the gas lasers being used require extensive development to achieve the high energy densities needed. Computer analysis is used to help understand the basic process and the many possible loss mechanisms. Potential energy curves must be computed, interpreted and used to study dynamic effects. Since most of the candidate laser systems are electron-beam or photolytically pumped, it is important to study electron-atom, electron-molecule and heavy particle scattering.

The foregoing applications are all examples of analytic work done on hydrodynamic systems consisting of interacting fluids subjected to a variety of external forces. Various interactions, such as particle transport processes, precipitation, material strength or electromagnetic fields, may differ among the systems, but the common underlying feature is the motion of fluids under the governing laws of hydrodynamics: the conservation of mass, momentum and energy. For example, at LLL it is estimated that more than half of the computational load for the computer can be characterized as hydrodynamic. The laws governing hydrodynamic interactions are usually expressed as a set of coupled partial differential equations, the solution of which is sought through finite difference approximations referred to a coordinate system, which may change position with time. Most of the hydrodynamic codes used contain numerical models of additional physical processes whose influence on the hydrodynamic behavior of the fluids is the main understanding to be developed.

Brockway and Gama-Lobo [1979] carried out a major vectorization effort on a large 2D Lagrangian hydrodynamic code that was the largest consumer of computer time at LANL. They achieved a tenfold running speed improvement over the CDC 7600 and a fourfold improvement over the CRAY-1 scalar code. Another code development of general interest for hydrodynamics problems has been the adaptive grid method of Dwyer et al. [1979]. For computer solution of transport equations, the method adaptively adjusts the grid spacing for independent variables to the rates of change in the dependent variables. Applied to flame propagation, which can include strong nonlinearities, the method reduced the number of required grid points and the computation time by an order of magnitude for the same accuracy of result.

New and Renewable Energy Resources

Photovoltaic cells provide one of the most eminently practicable ways of using solar energy. In these cells a semiconductor is treated with donor and acceptor material in adjacent regions, such that light within the solar emission spectrum excites electrons from the valence to the conduction band so that current flows between electrodes attached to the adjacent regions. The efficiency of the device in using solar energy depends on the probabilities for such transitions when it is exposed to sunlight in its operating environment. Terrestrial photovoltaic devices have available a lower intensity, and a smaller, more irregular spectrum of solar radiance than those placed on a satellite above the atmosphere. The transition probabilities for the available spectrum of light depend on the shapes in wave-vector space of the Brillouin zones for the valence and conduction band. A central issue in developing photovoltaic cells is the formulation of semiconductor compounds with the best Brillouin zone properties.

Orvis and Yee [1981] developed a computer modeling system that can be used to investigate a speculative semiconductor compound, determine the structure of its valence and conductive bands, and infer the main properties of photovoltaic cells fabricated from such a compound. The course of analysis is shown in Figure 2-4. From the band structure are calculated the band gap and the reduced masses of the charge carriers. With this and a model of the solar photovoltaic cell are calculated spectral response, current/voltage characteristic, fill factor and efficiency. The model also determines the sensitivity of the cell's characteristics to changes in the input parameters of impurity levels, geometry, resistivity, interface and surface recombination velocities, and grain size. The interface between grains acts as a strong trapping center, causing recombination of holes and electrons.

Environmental Study of Pollutant Uptake

Physical systems that involve chemical kinetics and dynamic transport processes are central features in modeling how pollution diffuses through the atmosphere. Theoretical models for these systems are usually represented by a set of coupled nonlinear partial differential equations expressing conservation laws for the physical variable of interest. The various systems of partial differential equations, although similar in structure, will differ in mathematical consequences due to differences in physical domain of interest and the approximations representing detailed molecular and atomic processes. The inclusion of chemical kinetics not only increases the number of equations to be solved (by 2–20X), but introduces greater nonlinearity and the "stiffness" problem. "Stiffness" refers to the presence of processes with widely differing time scales, which can add considerable computational requirement for the model. LLL developed several atmospheric models for applied research in atmospheric pollution. In addition to relevant atmospheric motion, the photochemistry of active pollutants may also be described. The models usually include 10–20 nonlinear partial differential equations with a fairly large physical domain of interest.

A general-purpose code to handle problems in chemical kinetics has been developed by Kee et al. [1981]. After the chemical reaction is

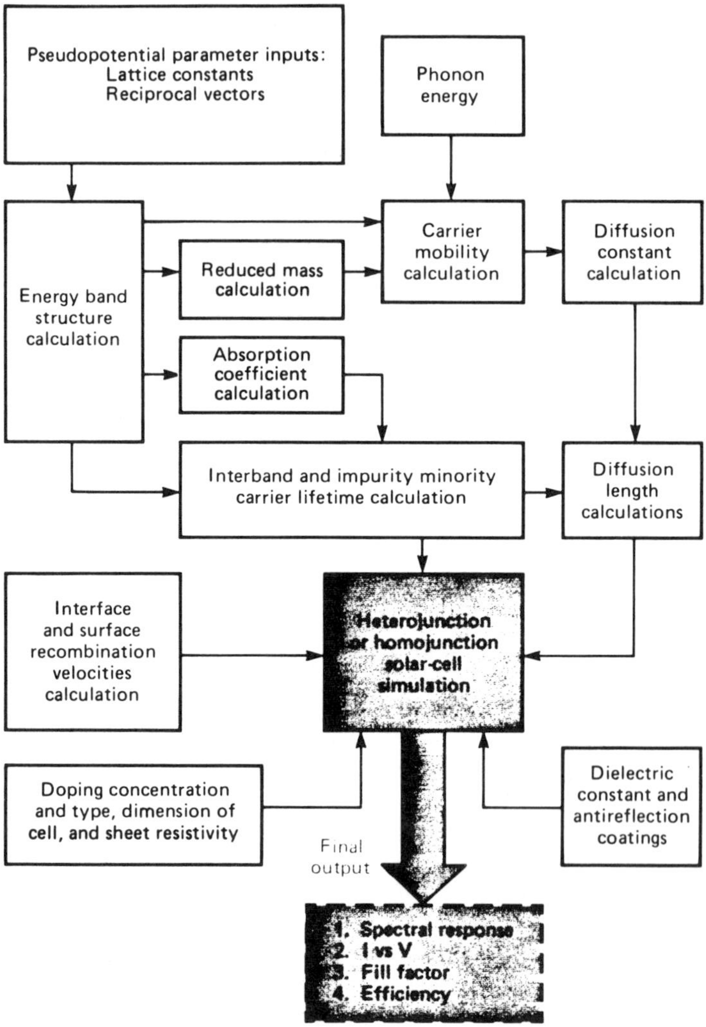

Figure 2-4. Flowchart of subroutines used to calculate material parameters of semiconducting materials and performance of solar cells made from them [Orvis and Yee 1981].

specified, the program accesses, according to user specification, modular subroutines that return thermodynamic properties, chemical production rates, equation-of-state variables, their derivatives and a variety of sensitivity parameters. The code was an outgrowth of earlier development of a chemical kinetic model of reduction of nitric oxide by ammonia [Branch et al. 1981; Miller et al. 1981].

Atmosphere and Ocean Dynamics

Numerical models of atmosphere and ocean dynamics are based on primitive equations of fluid motion taking into account transport of heat, moisture (in the case of atmospheres), boundary-layer effects and radiation. In particular, a major goal of climatic research has been the coupling of general global circulation models for the atmosphere and oceans to achieve possibly more accurate forecasts over a longer time period. The early development of numerical simulations in this area started with limited-domain atmospheric research models in the late 1940s and early 1950s. The prototype for modern general circulation models was developed in the early 1960s [Manabe et al. 1965; Smagorinsky et al. 1965], using a grid with nine vertical levels. Vertical grid resolution, relative amounts of computer time allowed for various parts of the problem, and the treatment of radiation, moisture convection, boundary-layer turbulence and energy dissipation in the free atmosphere are all comparable to similar features of the general circulation models in current use. After demonstration of some validity of long-term integration of the primitive equation atmospheric models, these techniques were applied to ocean circulation and the two areas thereafter developed in parallel.

Early extended prediction experiments with general circulation models include the two-week forecast by Miyakoda et al. [1969]. However, this is probably a limit imposed by the relatively sparse network of meteorological observation available at any one time as initial conditions. This has been confirmed at GFDL by two-week predictions for 12 January and 12 July cases, which required 13 years to complete between 1967 and 1980. Measurable predictive capacity was demonstrated for up to 10 days in the layers up to 500 mbars of atmospheric pressure (5800 m). Work has begun on extending this prediction range for subplanetary-scale anomalies, ignoring rapidly moving cyclones. Physical effects (such as latent heat release, and boundary-layer exchange of moisture and energy) become more important as the length of the forecast increases. The effects of ocean circulation will be important, and a seasonally varying global ocean-atmosphere model has been developed [Manabe et al. 1979]. Some recent work in this area has yielded some preliminary results concerning the unusually cold January of 1977 over North America. One of the models being tried, known as N48L9-E4, has been successful in predicting the lower-than-normal January temperature contours as shown in Figure 2-5 [GFDL 1980].

At GLAS, a nine-level general circulation model has been converted [Marx 1979] to run in a vectorized mode on the CDC STAR-100 available at NASA Langley Center. This resulted in an overall speed factor improvement of 4.5X over the same program run on the Amdahl

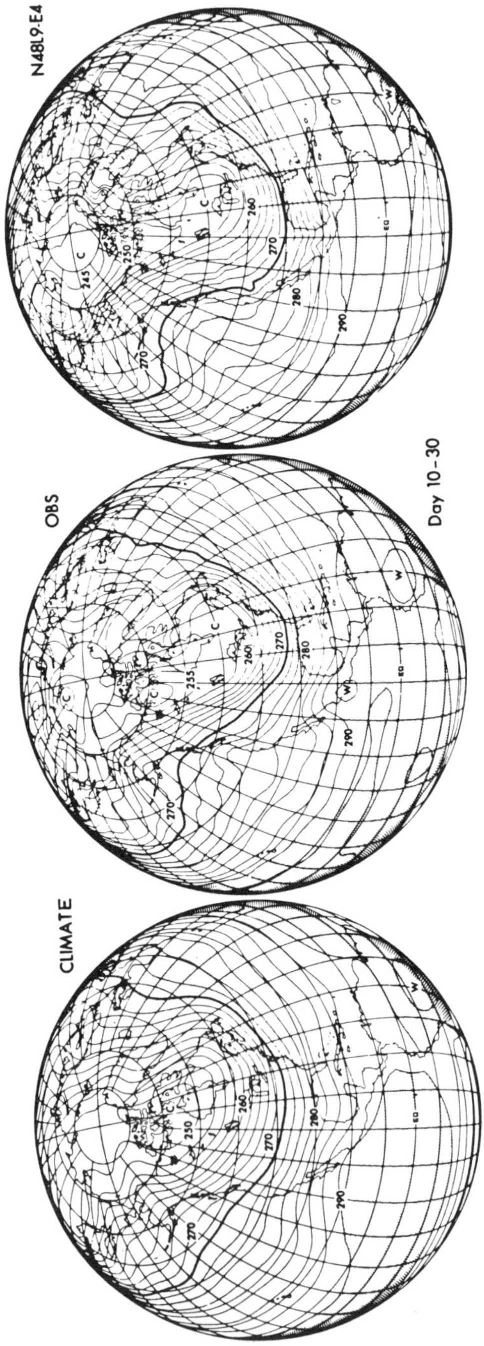

Figure 2.5. Comparison of temperatures for January 10–30, 1977. Left: normal (CLIMATE). Center: actual (OBS). Right: predicted by global circulation model (N48L9-E4) [GFDL 1980].

470 V/6. Weather prediction using general circulation models is carried out at GLAS in conjunction with the NASA program of developing satellite-based meteorological instrumentation. Cane et al. [1981] studied the sensitivity of prediction to satellite-sensed data on marine surface winds. The effects of error in the wind data, as initial conditions, were found to be substantial in degrading the predictive capability of the model. The largest effect was for surface winds as opposed to those sensed at higher levels. A more comprehensive assessment of the value of the FGGE satellite observing system has been carried out [Halem et al. 1981].

TYPICAL COMPUTATION REQUIREMENTS OF USER ORGANIZATIONS CONTACTED FOR DETAILED SURVEYS

Of the 16 organizations identified in Table 2-1, 7 agreed to extended discussion concerning their current or prospective application of the advanced computer being acquired and their experience in the selection process and early trials:

1. LLL, Livermore, California;
2. NMFECC, Livermore, California;
3. LANL, Los Alamos, New Mexico;
4. Sandia National Laboratory, Livermore, California;
5. Sandia National Laboratory, Albuquerque, New Mexico;
6. GLAS, NASA; and
7. GFDL, Princeton University.

Subsequent sections summarize briefly the kind of computational requirements perceived at these organizations as being most relevant to the selection of a vector processing computer. In addition to the subject matter of the applications, examples of which have been described above, they have all felt it is just as important to consider the way in which their personnel develop and use the programs executed on the computer.

Lawrence Livermore National Laboratory

At LLL, there is a broad range of interest (as shown in Table 2-1). Within computer applications, modeling normal fission reactor operations commands a relatively small effort. There are more substantial efforts in reactor safety estimates, modeling waste disposal strategies and the fuel cycle, and considerable work associated with modeling fusion processes in the development program for laser or inertial confinement. However, the pace of new computer code development is relatively slow compared to aggregate computer use. Most of the mathematical routines used are packaged. These usually are procedures for solving difference equations representing differential equations of motion for hydrodynamic, chemical and nuclear interactions. If at all possible, the scientific investigators avoid developing new algorithms in favor of using, or possibly adapting, an existing routine that can serve, even if without optimal efficiency. In most cases, the use of the package is part of a development program that does not lead to a substantial new code that would be in wide use later. There is little individual incentive to undertake the revisions required to vectorize the kernels of the code. LLL has chosen the CRAY computer, acquiring three so far. Primarily, only the advantage in faster scalar processing is being realized.

National Magnetic Fusion Energy Computer Center

Two CRAY computer systems are used almost exclusively for modeling the plasma phenomena of magnetically confined thermonuclear fusion. Several examples have been described above. There are also studies of safeguards for magnetic fusion reactors, systems for nonelectric application of fusion and some environmental studies. In contrast to LLL, most of the programs are developed in-house. They are used for a short time before being superseded by other newly developed programs. Moreover, through the NMFECC network, other laboratories with similar program-developing patterns, such as Oak Ridge National Laboratory (ORNL) and Princeton Plasma Physics Laboratory, use the CRAY systems. Certain standard algorithms developed at NMFECC for mathematical processes and some engineering problems associated with large magnetic fusion experiments have become used widely. There is little resort to outside packaged routines.

Los Alamos National Laboratory

A portion of the work of the LANL computing division pertains to fusion energy research and current problems in fission reactor operation, safety, waste management, fuel cycle and safeguards. Some work is associated with new and renewable energy sources, but usually with respect to physics calculations, such as noted above, rather than as solutions to design problems for large engineering projects. One of the major difficulties experienced in vectorizing programs for execution on the three CRAY systems presently installed arises in the high proportion of Monte Carlo calculations that are used to obtain statistical results.

Efficient operation of a vectorized code is hampered by the lack of special gather/scatter instructions, such as those of the CDC CYBER 205 (see Chapter 5). A particular problem faced in simulating fusion plasma phenomena is the large number of algorithms using nested subscripts for functional arguments. There is no general way to vectorize these for the CRAY system. Almost all of the application programs are run without revision for vectorization because of the excessive time this would take during the course of program development.

Sandia National Laboratory, Livermore, California

The Sandia laboratories are oriented more strictly toward immediately applicable technology development than are LLL and LANL. Sandia—Livermore emphasizes nuclear reactor safety, new and renewable energy resources and some environmental studies in scientific computer applications. They have one CRAY system. Most of the programs have been developed by the laboratory staff with about 5% purchased from outside sources. Heavy repeated production work is done only in structural analysis and heat dynamics. A broad range of technical problems are treated with analysis that generally consists of the solution of systems of linear differential equations. Three subjects were cited as examples of the scientific work:

1. fission reactors: Monte Carlo calculation of neutron damage to reactor vessel material, and fundamental study of defects in solids (such as interaction energy of hydrogen atoms placed in interstitial positions);
2. renewable energy: Monte Carlo calculations of energy losses in central solar receiver mirror fields; and
3. environment: generation of pollutants by fossil fuel burning using laser light transmission diagnostic techniques.

Sandia National Laboratory, Albuquerque, New Mexico

Sandia—Albuquerque is very similar to Sandia—Livermore in its computer operations. The computer division's equipment includes one CRAY system. Its applications emphasize nuclear reactor safety, nuclear waste disposal and alternative energy resources. In connection with Sandia's development of the electron beam fusion accelerator EBFA-1, a large modeling program for inertial confinement fusion is also carried on. There is a somewhat higher proportion of outside developed programs being used, usually those developed by other DOE laboratories and NRC.

Three specific areas of computational analysis were cited as most in need of the CRAY system capability:

1. RELAP programs to analyze severe departures from normal reactor operation;
2. fault tree analysis of reactor accidents; and
3. numerical simulation of explosive fracturing for oil shale retorting.

Goddard Laboratory for Atmospheric Science, NASA

A major emphasis in the science work at GLAS is to increase the utility of satellite-based instrumentation for data that can improve weather prediction. There is continued use of a general circulation model that was developed earlier with the Goddard Institute for Space Studies. The laboratory anticipated the installation of a CDC CYBER 205 in summer 1982. With it they hoped to use smaller spatial divisions and time steps in the general circulation model. In addition, the increased capacity would be used to analyze data from the entire NASA meteorological network for synoptic presentations over very wide areas. Model development proceeds much more slowly than at the energy laboratories, so that there would be repeated production runs for new meteorological data sets.

Geophysical Fluid Dynamics Laboratory

The computational work at GFDL is similar to that at GLAS; there is heavy emphasis on using general circulation models. However, there is no hard linkage to promoting instrumentation development. Instead, there is more emphasis on further elaboration of the physical effects being incorporated into the model. Characteristically, the major problems of atmospheric processes and ocean-atmosphere interactions are studied using a large number of different models to compare their predictive capabilities. In this way, some understanding of the relative importance of the different physical effects is gained according to the way in which they are represented in the models. GFDL has been using the Texas Instruments vector processor TIX 4 AJC since 1974. A CDC CYBER 205 was selected to replace it in fall 1982.

USER EVALUATION OF VECTOR PROCESSING COMPUTERS

The individual responses of the foregoing users contacted for detailed interviews are described comprehensively in Chapter 6. In the following sections, their collective experience is summarized for the main issues that might be confronted by a prospective user of vector/parallel processing systems in the near future.

Common Advantages for Vector/Parallel Processors

For computer application areas that place heavy demands on the computer system, users perceive a high value for cost-effective computation. These applications occupy mainly the central arithmetic processor rather than the I/O channels of the computer system. Because typical problems require high throughput rates on very structured data, the high computation rates of the CRAY and CDC vector processing systems provide greater cost-effectiveness than do conventional general-purpose computers. One very important issue is the extent of time that can be dedicated to one program for one long run, typically overnight. This was widely perceived as 20 hours. If a meaningful computation takes longer, greater computational capacity is required or all other users of the computer center suffer delays in their programs. Similar motivations were also expressed by some prospective users of the Denelcor HEP parallel processor, which is somewhat slower but less expensive.

A second important advantage mentioned by most of the users is the large rapid-access main memory that is available on vector/parallel processing systems. This not only allows large arrays to be handled efficiently, without resort to auxiliary storage and extra I/O operations, but also relieves constraints on the complexity of the program that must be kept in the main memory.

Common Problems with Vector/Parallel Processors

Two problems were mentioned by representatives of all the users: (1) the need to revise programs to take full advantage of vector processing capability; and (2) the low level of software support for systems and general utility applications.

The work needed to vectorize a FORTRAN program is considered so great that only critical portions of long-established production codes are being modified. For investigators involved in program development, the return in reduced run charges is too low compared to the considerable time they would spend vectorizing a program that may be run only a few times before wholesale changes are required. The most energetic program vectorization effort has been that of the LANL group. These staff members are in the computer division and do not carry out any specific large program (10,000 lines). For a large program (100,000 lines), modifying it to get 90% vector utilization would require 50 man-years of effort.

The low level of software support has been anticipated by all the users and dismissed as a minor factor in their selection deliberations. One exception is the CRAY research FORTRAN compiler, which its users considered better than all others. Practically all of the user organizations have computer center staff capability to develop or modify specialized system, and acquiring the Amdahl 5860 presents no problem, for which they can rely a great deal on IBM system software as well as application programs written in PL/I. The Weapons Laboratory, choosing the CRAY-1S, intends to rely wholly on the FORTRAN compiler.

Specific Advantages and Problems

Since practically all of the user experience is with the CRAY systems, there is much more and better substantiated information for them. The advantages and problems of the CDC CYBER 205 and Denelcor HEP have been discerned only in terms of the benchmark tests that led to their selection.

CRAY-1S

Three major advantages are cited by the users. Program execution speed averages about four times better than that of the CDC 7600. However, the improvement factor varys widely between about 1.75 and >10, depending on how well the kernel algorithms can be vectorized. The speed advantage can also be surpassed in some cases by the CDC CYBER 205. For example, the exemplary programs used by GLAS and GFDL in their benchmark procurement tests were handled faster by the CDC CYBER 205. Reliability in terms of minimal down time required for both routine and exceptional maintenance is, by all the testimony, superior for the CRAY systems. Availability can be expected to average 93–96% after allocation of 3–8 hr/week for preventive maintenance. This user testimony conflicts a little with statements by McCraney [1981], who suggests no more than 4 hr/week. Finally, there is the apparently superb FORTRAN compiler available from CRAY. A number of the investigators pointed out that their compilation times, compared to those of other compilers working on the same programs, were reduced by as much as 40X. Frequently, in a course of program development, compilation time used to be greater than run time. The extremely fast compiler has therefore greatly facilitated and reduced the cost of program development.

The single major problem with the CRAY-1S is the lack of any time-sharing provision in their available system software. As a result, the energy laboratories have developed their own time-sharing system operated with the networks connecting centrally located CRAY with remotely located laboratories engaged in DOE research. A minor problem is the special Freon® cooling system, which requires fairly noisy compressors located in separate rooms and doubles required electric power.

CDC CYBER 205

The main advantage of the CDC CYBER 205 is very high speed when the kernel algorithm can be vectorized with very long vectors [Bucher and Moore 1981]. This is probably true in simulating atmospheres and oceans for purposes of weather prediction. There are no Monte Carlo calculations and, using the CDC CYBER 205, very fine-meshed grids can be used if one is careful to sequence properly, to provide aggregates of independent similar arithmetic operations.

The major problem of the CDC CYBER 205 is the lack of software support, including, most importantly, a FORTRAN compiler with vector diagnostic capability. Actual reliability of the system is still unknown, but CDC will commit to a standard GSA contract availability factor of 90% with about 8 hr/week of preventive maintenance [Kneisly 1981].

Denelcor HEP

The Denelcor HEP will apparently supply faster scalar processing than the CDC 7600; however, without adding multiprocessing capability with extra modules, it will not approach the execution speeds of the CRAY-1S and CDC CYBER 205 systems. A major problem area anticipated is lack of software support, since the Denelcor organization is much smaller even than those of Cray Research and CDC. Data on hardware reliability will probably not be available for at least a year.

Experience of User Organizations with Working Systems

Only the CRAY systems have been installed long enough for an appreciable accumulation of practical user experience. The following sections summarize the most significant points cited by the users for their CRAY systems. Their testimony is related in more detail in Chapter 6.

System Installation and Service

Unanimously, the users contacted for detailed interviews expressed great satisfaction with both hardware and software installation service. The processors, with associated peripheral hardware, arrived almost exactly on schedule and the Cray Research staff had little difficulty incorporating the equipment into the users' existing networks. There was also ample support provided by Cray Research analysts in converting existing programs and operating software. The LANL group has the longest experience with CRAY systems; they report that the time required for design, preparation and final installation has been reduced from six months for their first system in 1976 to eight weeks for the latest 1981 systems.

Available Hardware

CRAY supplies only the central processing unit, the CRAY-1S. It may be equipped with 0.5, 1 and 2 megawords (16 megabytes) of main memory. The user requires a front-end processor, which, in the case of the users contacted, was generally a CDC 6600 or 7600. Auxiliary disk storage up to 9.6 gigabytes was linked to a single processor (at NMFECC). The disk drives used were either the single-density D819 or double-density DD829 made by CDC. With the sophisticated communication networks used, a wide variety of other equipment was also linked. This included such high-capacity units as the Los Alamos Common File System mass memory (4.4 terabits) and high-speed (10,000 lines per minute) Xerox 9700 printers.

Available Software

All of the users expressed great satisfaction with the CRAY FORTRAN computer, but many did not use much of the system software because it did not include time-sharing and interactive capability. They implemented the CRAY Time Sharing System (CTSS) developed by the computing staff at NMFECC. One user pointed out that there is no CRAY PL/I computer available, nor is one likely in the near future. CRAY research is still a very small organization, with a staff of about 1000, and there is insufficient demand among their customers to warrant allocating the resources to develop a PL/I compiler.

General Commentary

The users were unanimously satisfied in general with the CRAY systems and most were planning additional units. There was concern expressed at the energy laboratories for any prospective user without their own considerable expertise in software design to compensate for Cray Research's deficiencies. However, the U.S. Air Force Weapon Laboratory acknowledged a much lower level of staff software design expertise, and nevertheless was satisfied overall with the increased computing capacity gained compared with the system's cost. One user regretted having acquired a CRAY-1 system with only a 0.5-megaword main memory. At least 1 megaword was considered advisable.

CHAPTER 3

OUTLOOK FOR IMPROVED VECTOR PROCESSOR HARDWARE CAPABILITY

Technical progress in vector/parallel processor hardware can be expected both in microelectronic technology and machine architectural design concepts. This section describes current trends in these areas and, where possible, indicates specific advances expected by the three major vendors of vector/parallel machines: Cray Research, Incorporated, Control Data Corporation (CDC) and Denelcor, Incorporated. The development of this generation of supercomputers is being driven by the computational requirements for advanced simulation models in fusion research and aerodynamics. In a program of sponsored development being considered by the National Aeronautics and Space Administration (NASA) for aerodynamics design computation [Kolata 1981], a new order or performance capability would be sought in the range of billions of floating point operations per second. The main vendors bidding on this program are CDC and Burroughs. At the Los Alamos National Scientific Laboratory (LANL), for long-range planning, the assumption has been made that by 1990 there will be available computational speed at least 10 times that of the CRAY-1S with 16 megawords of fast memory [Ewald et al. 1981]. To meet this challenge, the major vector/parallel processor manufacturers will implement machines with hardware capability based on a variety of innovative design concepts.

GENERAL TECHNOLOGICAL TRENDS

Evolution of the next generation of vector/parallel processors will be achieved primarily through a combined effort, using high technology in logic circuit design, notably very-large-scale integration (VLSI) and new multiprocessor architecture design concepts. This approach is necessary, because the leading edge of the state-of-the-art technology in microelectronics has begun to experience major difficulties in the design and manufacture of the highly complex logic chips for the next generation of processors. In addition, there are limitations inherent in the laws governing charge carrier migration through solids. Logic circuit components will not increase in speed by two orders of magnitude during this decade as they did in the last decade [Worlton 1981]. It has been shown, for example, that even the inclusion of Josephson junction circuits will not eliminate the advantage of the vector processing concept [Buzbee 1981]. However, both CDC and Denelcor intend to develop VLSI versions of their machines. Cray Research will move to medium-scale integration (MSI) technology from its current small-scale integration (SSI) mode.

Recognizing the limitations of advanced logic circuit technology, vector processor manufacturers have elected to use machine architectures based on a multiprocessor design concept. Both CDC and Cray Research will probably exploit the advantages of parallel processing in conjunction with vector processing. Cray Research is reputed to be considering a dual-processor version of the CRAY-1S to be followed by a four-processor architecture for the CRAY-2.

To complement the dramatic increase in computational speed in the main processor(s), main memory and peripheral storage devices with very high access speeds and bandwidth will also be required. Main memory will be much larger than presently available and with very high bandwidth. Except for the CRAY-2, the design of the new main memories will probably incorporate the 256K dynamic random-access memory (DRAM) chip if it becomes available in sufficient quantities.

Secondary storage will consist of two types: (1) very-high-speed and very-large-bandwidth fixed-disk devices; and (2) auxiliary semiconductor memory storage. The disk devices would be multiple parallel-head versions of currently available disk drives. Semiconductor memory will also be used in instances that require faster memory access time and higher bandwidth than are provided by fixed-disk storage devices. Cray Research will not develop disk drives, but will concentrate on the development of an auxiliary semiconductor memory.

SPECIFIC ADVANCES ANTICIPATED FOR VECTOR/PARALLEL PROCESSORS

CRAY-1S, -X/MP and -2

The research and development (R&D) program at Cray Research, Incorporated consists of two distinct development projects for enhanced computer performance and alternative architecture design concepts. Cray Research is committed to develop the best machine design by exploring many alternative technologies rather than committing to a single design concept. These efforts will result in an enhanced version of the CRAY-1S, the CRAY-X/MP, and will lead to the next generation of CRAY machines, the recently announced CRAY-2.

The CRAY-X/MP will be a dual-processor version of the CRAY-1S. Its design will incorporate emitter-coupled logic (ECL) technology based on MSI. However, large-scale integration (LSI) will be in evidence for the main memory. The enhancements are an upgrade to 16K ECL random-access memory (RAM) chips from the 4K variety currently used in the CRAY-1S. In addition, 16 gates per ECL array will be used as opposed to 2 gates currently used in the CRAY-1S. A 30% improvement in computational rate has been realized, i.e., a cycle time of 7–8 nsec for CRAY-X/MP [*Datamation* 1982]. In addition, the memory cycle time has been significantly reduced to 38 nsec and a 50-megaword auxiliary solid-state memory will be available for the CRAY-X/MP.

Cray Research is also continuing investigations into techniques of using state-of-the-art production technologies in electronics in conjunction with advanced cooling techniques to attain greater computational speed and size reduction without use of LSI technology. MSI will be used throughout to achieve high reliability and availability goals. The recently announced CRAY-2 is an example of a processor that will be based on this design strategy. This model is expected to be on the market within three to four years. It is expected to have 32 megawords of main memory and will exploit both parallelism and vector processing architectural concepts using four tightly coupled processors. [*Datamation* 1981].

ECL technology will still be used in the CRAY-2 at the level of MSI with 16 gates per ECL gate array. Main memory will use 16K ECL RAM. In contrast, the CRAY-1S used 2 gates per ECL gate array and 4K RAM. Switching performance will be 300–500 psec [*Datamation* 1982]. The CRAY-2 will have a 3- to 4-nsec cycle time and perform at a computation rate of 2800 million floating point operations per second (MFLOPS) in the vector mode and 1200 million instructions per second (MIPS) in the scalar mode [*Datamation* 1981]. It will be compatible with earlier Cray machines at the high-level language standard but not at the assembly language level. The longest wire length in the CRAY-2 circuitry will be 16 in. It will have a cylindrical frame structure 38 in. in diameter and 28 in. in height [*Datamation* 1982].

CRAY-2 circuitry will be three-dimensional with eight triangular boards per module in tetrahedral array. Each module is 1 in. in height. Twenty-six modules will be arranged in a stack. The circuits will be totally immersed in a circulating fluorocarbon liquid to meet the cooling requirements. The price range for the CRAY-2 is estimated as $10–20 million [*Datamation* 1982].

CDC CYBER 200 Model 205/CYBER 2XX

Specific information on the next generation of CYBER 200 series is currently unavailable. However, some general trends can be deduced. CDC will develop an enhanced version of the CYBER 200 Model 205 processor. This machine, temporarily designated as the CYBER 2XX, is expected to be commercially available by mid-1985 and actively compete with CRAY-2. The CYBER 2XX will probably incorporate VLSI in some or all aspects of its design. In addition, it is also expected to be based on tightly coupled multiprocessor architecture—a dual- or four-processor design. Computational performance in the vector mode would reach well into the billions of floating point operations per second [gigaflops (GFLOPS)] range, depending on the number of processors used in the design.

To match this magnitude of computational performance, very-high-speed secondary memory will be required. Secondary memory devices would be based on the multiple-head versions of current CDC fixed-disk storage devices and on the development of an auxiliary semiconductor memory. The secondary memory would be implemented with metal-oxide semiconductor (MOS) technology and could hold up to 32 million words at a cost of 10 cents per word [Levine 1981].

Denelcor Heterogeneous Element Processor (HEP)

Because of its recent arrival in the marketplace, extensive enhancements in HEP hardware capability are currently in the planning stage. Proposed enhancements will include a VLSI version of the HEP [Denelcor 1981a,b]. A main memory based on MOS technology is also planned for development [Belzer 1982]. The major thrust of HEP enhancements will be directed into system and application software.

CHAPTER 4

ANTICIPATED SOFTWARE DEVELOPMENT

Concurrent with the advances in hardware technology are programs for significant advances in system application software design and research into the structuring of simulation models to more readily use algorithms based on vectorization concepts. Denelcor, Control Data Corporation (CDC) and Cray Research, Incorporated have initiated very strong system software development efforts. CDC has taken the lead in exploring a variety of alternatives. Cray Research is the next strongest in this area, with its efforts concentrated in compiler and extensive application software. Due to a late arrival in the marketplace, Denelcor is pursuing an ambitious development program for both system and application software for their unique machine architecture.

GENERAL OUTLOOK FOR SOFTWARE DESIGN DEVELOPMENT

To support some of the new hardware design approaches, complex system software will also be developed. Emphasis will be placed on the development of highly optimized FORTRAN compilers with extended vector capabilities. Initial development efforts for new high-level programming languages that will aid the scientist in structuring his problem for vectorization concepts have begun to take place. There have also been significant advances in research in applied mathematics: algorithms and new mathematical techniques will take full computational advantage of the new machine architectures. For example, Barkai [1981] and Moriarity [1981] have been able to devise a vectored algorithm for a lattice gauge theory calculation that includes Monte Carlo iterations.

SPECIFIC SOFTWARE DEVELOPMENTS

CRAY-1S

Future enhancements to the current system software for the CRAY-1S will include a highly optimized FORTRAN compiler with enhanced automatic vectorization capabilities. This compiler will provide a greater degree of vectorization for conditional code. A 15% average increase in vectorization performance will be realized over the current version of the CRAY FORTRAN compiler. The new compiler was scheduled for release during the early part of 1982 [Berlin 1982]. Application software released during 1982 [Hippe 1981] includes an extensive library of scientific subroutines and a vectorized version of NASTRAN for the CRAY-1S.

CRAY-2

Detailed information on system software for the CRAY-2 is currently unavailable. However, general information indicates that high-level language compatibility will be preserved for user developed application software. Compatibility at the assembly language level will not be preserved.

CDC CYBER 205

Enhancements to current system software for the CYBER 205 include:

1. a new FORTRAN compiler compatible with ANSI X3.9–1978, scheduled for release by mid-1982;
2. additional front-end support to provide interactive capability through the CYBER Remote Host Facility software, and UNIVAC and IBM operating under MVT with ASP and TSO; and
3. continual improvement of the CYBER VSOS 200 virtual storage operating system.

CDC CYBER 2XX

A major effort is expected in the development of system software for the CYBER 2XX. The major thrust of system software development should center on:

1. An improved ANSI standard FORTRAN compiler with extensions will provide a greater degree of automatic vectorization. These extensions will consist of machine instructions for the vector related operations SCATTER, GATHER, WHERE, ENDWHERE, OTHERWISE and SETRANGE. SCATTER instructions will take

vector elements in contiguous memory locations and scatter them into specified addresses directed by a vector containing the target addresses. GATHER instruction will take elements from noncontiguous locations and gather them into contiguous locations within memory at addresses supplied by a separate address vector. WHERE, ENDWHERE and OTHERWISE syntax denotes structured code blocks to be executed under specific conditions. SETRANGE will provide for vector construct obtained from the slicing of multidimensional grids.

2. Programming at the machine language level will be discouraged for the CYBER 2XX. However, a new high-level programming language compiler will probably be introduced. It will be a highly structured language specifically designed for the scientist.

In addition to these efforts, a versatile operating system software will be developed to support both multiprogramming and multiprocessing environments.

Denelcor HEP

Denelcor's efforts will be concentrated in the development of system and application software. An improved version of the HEP FORTRAN IV compiler will be available within the near term. The current HEP FORTRAN compiler is compatible with ANSI X3.9–1966 (FORTRAN 66) and a new FORTRAN compiler, compatible with ANSI X3.9–1978, is to be available in 1982.

At present, parallel process implementation must be explicitly introduced by the programmer through special FORTRAN syntax. Development of an automatic parallel processing feature that will provide program segmentation into parallel processes is underway. The first features of such implementation were to be available in 1981. A version of NASTRAN application software is being developed by the University of Georgia for the HEP [Belzer 1982].

CHAPTER 5

VECTOR AND PARALLEL PROCESSOR SYSTEMS

This chapter explains the distinctive features that determine exactly how the streams of data and instructions of a computer program are handled in the new high-speed computers. The first section describes vector and parallel processing concepts and how these are reflected in the design of currently available systems, CRAY-1S, Control Data Corporation (CDC) CYBER Model 205 and Denelcor Heterogeneous Element Processor (HEP). Additionally, the design of the Amdahl 580 series is also included to present a very fast conventional alternative. The second section describes the main features of the hardware implementation of these basic designs and presents some comparison of the main operational features of the complete systems.

VECTOR AND PARALLEL PROCESSING

There are two main approaches to raising significantly the operational speed of computers. One is to improve the electronic design or incorporate new physical principles in the system hardware to sharply reduce the time it takes for signals to travel among the circuit elements. Current possibilities in this direction are considered to be a decade away from realization in the United States. The second approach is to change the way data and instructions are handled in computers so as to have simultaneous operation of many instructions in a program. This is the approach of the highest-speed currently available U.S. systems, those using the vector and parallel processing concepts.

It is not always possible to use simultaneous execution of a sequence of programmed arithmetic operations, since successive steps frequently depend on immediately preceding results. However, there are many computations, such as operations on very large matrices or spectral analysis, for which most of the computational execution time is consumed in carrying out a long sequence of independent instructions. Also, since the early advent of vector/parallel processing in predecessor systems such as the CDC STAR and Texas Instruments ASC, a number of computational physicists have succeeded in modifying the underlying computational algorithms for other kinds of calculations so that they can be expressed in a computer program that takes advantage of simultaneous execution of instructions [Buzbee et al. 1977]. Additionally, high-level languages are being developed to enhance the capability of vector processor compilers to automatically vectorize computer programs.

Vector and parallel processor designs represent two approaches to achieving simultaneous execution of a sequence of instructions. Both designs include provision for assembling a long series of data operands in fast-access registers that act as auxiliaries to the main memory. In this way the operands can be moved rapidly to the arithmetic operation modules to be coordinated with rapid execution of instructions on a data sequence. The designs differ in their provisions for simultaneous execution of instructions. The parallel processor adds more arithmetic operation modules, so that operands may be operated on in parallel. This entails certain supervisory provisions, such as monitoring processor occupancy, to assure smooth flow of the programming steps. In the vector processor, on the other hand, a single arithmetic operation module is segmented so that an instruction is carried out in a pipeline of independent steps, each step timed in accordance with the basic cycle time of the processor. Arrayed variables are placed in special vector registers and handled somewhat differently from other variables, which are termed scalar and placed in scalar registers. A sequence of sets of operands taken from the vector and scalar registers will move through the pipelined operation, each set progressing through the independent segmented steps. For example, if the operation has been broken down into eight steps, then eight sets of operands may be processed simultaneously to achieve the same ultimate improvement as a purely parallel processor with eight arithmetic operation modules.

The currently marketed vector/parallel processor computers are divided into two groups:

1. CRAY-1S and CDC CYBER 205 are oriented toward vector processing, which is also termed single-instruction multiple-data (SIMD) stream central processing unit (CPU) architecture.
2. Denelcor HEP is based almost purely on parallel processing, which is also termed multiple-instruction multiple-data (MIMD) stream.

The following sections describe further some of the differences and similarities among these systems in further details of the design of their central processing units.

VECTOR INSTRUCTION PROCESSING

As examples of SIMD CPU architecture, the CRAY-1S and CDC CYBER 205 both contain pipeline vector arithmetic processors capable of performing operations on arrays at very high speeds. In addition, each has a scalar processor subdivided into several functional units capable of performing a variety of operations, concurrently with each other and with the vector pipeline units. These operations may take place in precisions of 32 or 64 bits for both scalar and vector operands. In the CRAY-1S, vector operations are performed on operands drawn from eight rapid-access vector registers, each 64 elements (all up to 64 bits) long. In the CDC CYBER Model 205, vector operands are arrayed in stream units that consist of a set of sequential elements (each up to 64 bits), numbering up to 65,536, that are rapidly accessed through a high-speed register memory interface.

CRAY-1S Vector Processing

Primary general operating registers of the CRAY-1S are the scalar and vector registers as shown in Figure 5-1 [Kolodzey 1981]. The eight S registers contain one element each and the eight V registers contain 64 elements each. An instruction, such as addition, obtains its operands from these registers and places the result in an unoccupied register. Sets of input operands for repeated execution are taken in each clock period, which is 12.5 nsec [Johnson 1978].

Arithmetic, logical and shift operations are carried out by the 12 specialized functional units shown at the right edge of Figure 5-1. Each unit is independent of the others and may be in operation at the same time. For a sequence of instructions that involves separately independent units, such as add and multiply, it is possible to operate in the manner of a parallel processor. Primarily, though, execution speed is obtained by full segmentation of each functional unit. Information arriving at the unit or moving within it is captured and held in a new set of registers at the end of each clock period. Hence, a new set of operands for unrelated computation may be started into a functional unit each clock period, even though the unit may require several clock periods to complete the calculation.

Vector instructions provide advance scheduling of system resources for

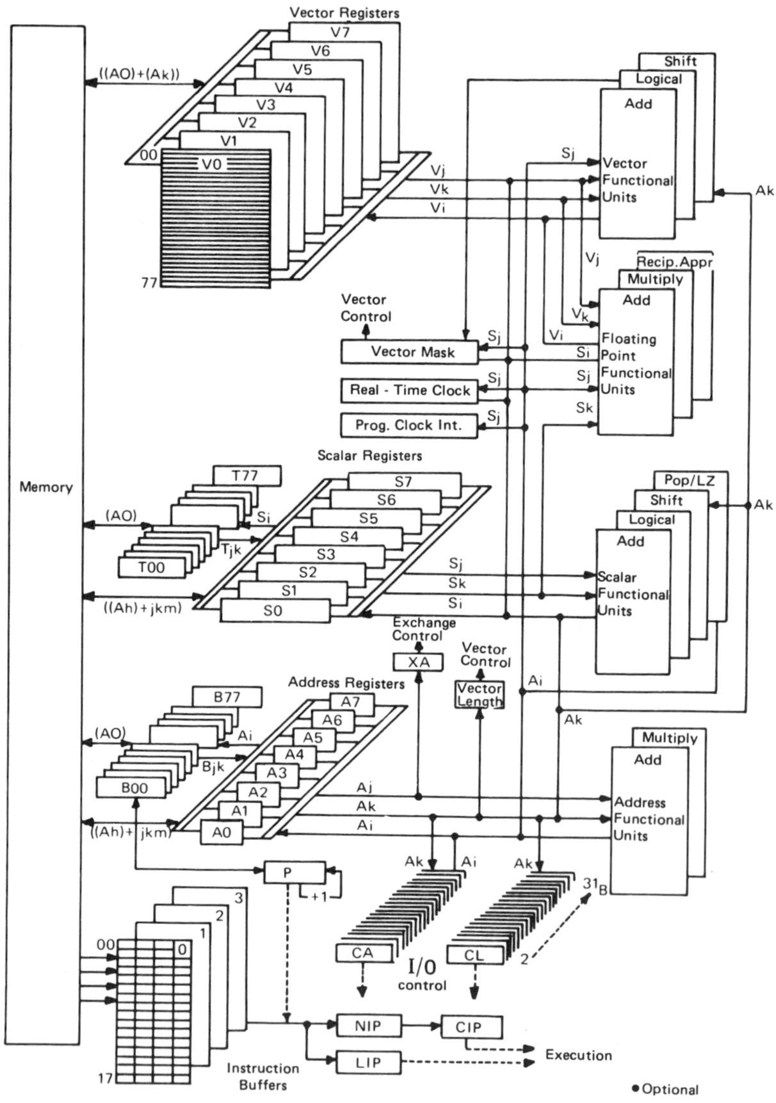

Figure 5-1. CRAY-1S computation [Kolodzey 1981].

such calculations by placing reservations on the required functional units, memory and input operand registers. Associated with every vector instruction is an initial functional unit. A startup delay may occur equal to four clock periods plus the vector length in clock periods of any preceding vector operation [Russell 1978].

Vector operations that depend on a previous result may be "chained" if the previous operation is done on an independent functional unit. When a vector instruction is issued, the result register is reserved for the number of clock periods determined by the vector length and functional unit time. A result register becomes the operand register of a succeeding instruction. This succeeding instruction is issued as soon as the first result arrives. That particular clock period, termed "chain slot time," occurs only once for each vector instruction. If the succeeding instruction cannot start operating at chain slot time because of a prior functional unit or operand register reservation, it must wait until the result register reservation is released [Russell 1978].

Chaining is parallel processing adjunct to the pipelining concept whereby different functional units may be linked to produce a result as input for further computation. A maximum delay occurs during this process up to the chain slot time, which is determined (in number of clock periods) as two plus the functional unit time. The CRAY operating system automatically performs chaining, although the programmer can influence the extent to which it occurs. It is possible for all functional units to be chained during the performance of a multiple-step operation. Under most conditions, however, no more than four functional units are chained [Auerbach 1981a-g].

Intermediate results are stored in a vector register, and a separate instruction is required to store the final result in memory. The vector register capacity is 64 elements. Vector lengths greater than 64 are processed in 64-element segments. An example of timings for both scalar and vector computation modes is presented in the next section.

Vectorization provides a major advantage in the execution of code for FORTRAN DO loops. The CRAY-1S FORTRAN compiler (CFT) optimizes the code and automatically vectorizes innermost DO loops with certain limitations. Vectorization of a DO loop will occur automatically if the DO loop executes operations on arrays and stores the results of computations in arrays. Loop structures that contain branch statements, conditional IF statements or subroutine calls are not currently vectorized by the CFT. However, these loop types may be vectorized by the inclusion of special vector statements. CRAY plans future versions of the compiler that will be able to vectorize loops of this kind to whatever extent allowed by the logic of the program.

CDC CYBER 205 Vector Processing

The CYBER 200 Model 205 processes long vectors in sections up to 65,536 64-bit elements [CDC 1980]. Optimum performance is achieved if the vectors are stored in contiguous locations. The CYBER 205 vector instructions reference memory directly. As shown in Figure 5-2, the vector processing unit may contain one, two or four parallel, segmented, floating point pipelines to facilitate high-speed vector processing. Control of the vector processor is provided by the stream unit, which controls, buffers and manipulates single-word operands and bit strings to and from memory. Single-word operands are available to the floating point pipelines every 20 nsec (in contrast to 12.5 nsec for CRAY-1S). Parallel operation of floating point units can be achieved during vector processing when two or four pipelines process alternate segments of the data stream. Bit string and logic operations are performed in the string unit, which receives operands from the stream unit and is dedicated to Boolean operations performed on arbitrary sets of bits.

In addition to the primitive arithmetic functional units for vector add, vector subtract, vector multiply and vector divide, the CYBER 205 has a dedicated vector square-root arithmetic unit and a special triadic functional unit called a vector-linked multiply and add or subtract. Triadic operations are performed on a combination of two input vector streams and one input scalar stream, as for the following two examples:

1. vector + scalar × vector, and
2. (vector + scalar) × vector.

Such operations are performed as a single sequence of segments through the triadic functional unit rather than having to be pipelined in sequence through separate add and multiply functional units.

Floating point operations are performed in the CYBER 205 by one-, two- and four-pipeline configurations. Each pipeline is capable of performing 32- and 64-bit floating point add, subtract, multiply, divide and square-root operations. Performance comparison of 64-bit operands in both scalar and vector modes for a two-pipeline configuration are presented below.

Vectorization of FORTRAN DO loop structures is not performed automatically by the CYBER 200 FORTRAN compiler, but must be invoked by options in the CYBER 200 job control language. Programmers may also use FORTRAN extensions that provide direct access to hardware capabilities for vector and string manipulation.

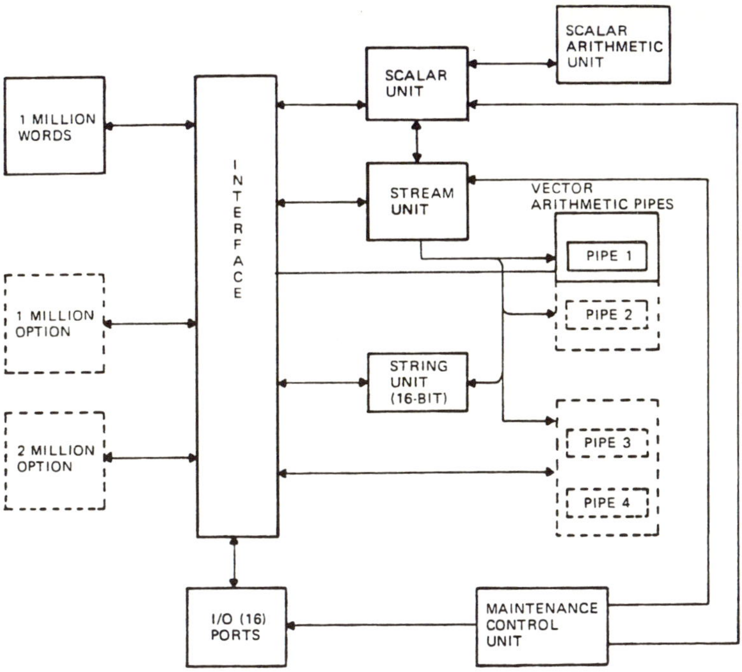

Figure 5-2. CDC CYBER 205 system configuration [CDC 1980].

Parallel Processing

The Denelcor HEP design is based on a MIMD stream CPU architecture. It is a typical parallel processor. Computational efficiency is achieved through a number of high-speed scalar processors that can execute a large number of programs independently in either a single program or multiprogramming process execution modules (PEM). The HEP word length is 64 bits. All data memory modules and processors are interconnected by a high-speed data switch network. All data memory is accessible by all PEM. A single user's program may be arranged as several processes. These processes, executing in parallel in one or more PEM, may interact by reading and writing shared information in data memory, so that the program is executed with the combined speed of all the processors being used [Denelcor 1981a,b].

Data flow is governed by use of a full/empty attribute for each memory location. Instruction execution control is assured by a communications discipline that allows instruction execution on input data memory locations in a "full" state, and leaves the location "empty" during the postexecution mode. Similarly, output locations in memory are "empty" before execution and "full" after execution. The full/empty attribute provides integrity of interprocess variables. For memory locations used exclusively within a process, the full/empty attribute is ignored and unrestricted memory access is provided in this instance.

Software modules in both FORTRAN and assembler languages may be distributed across several PEM to achieve maximum throughput capability. The design of a parallel program is not affected by whether the program will run in one or several PEM.

The HEP FORTRAN compiler provides extensions that enable the programmer to create and terminate parallel processes within a program. Processes may be created at any point in a program and terminated when their function is completed. Up to 64 user processes may exist concurrently within each PEM. It is planned that later versions of the HEP FORTRAN compiler will provide automatic parallelism for FORTRAN programs.

Because of this high degree of parallelism, two types of calculations are ideally suited for the Denelcor HEP:

1. Large systems of ordinary or partial differential equations that result from the simulation of continuous systems: heat transfer and fluid dynamics problems have this property. Vector operations are difficult to apply in this instance because of the constraints for these equations based on immediately prior results.
2. Partial differential equations in which the adjacent element states of the discrete elements in the model change rapidly: free surface, fractional distillation simulations and particle electrodynamics applications have this property.

HIGH-CAPACITY CONVENTIONAL ARCHITECTURE

The Amdahl 580 is a single-instruction single-data (SISD) stream processor that was scheduled for market arrival in April 1982. It is available in single- and dual-processor configurations. This computer system has been included as a comparison item in this study because it represents the most powerful machine in this class and may occasionally be selected as an alternative to vector/parallel processors. As a conventional processor, its high computational performance is due to use of pipelining in fetching operands and instructions, large-scale integration (LSI) logic, and hardwired assembly language macrocode. A key design feature is its compatibility with the IBM/370 operating system. Application software has been developed under the IBM/370 operating system series: MVS/SP Releases 1, 2 and 3; VM/SP Release 1, and ACP can run without modification.

PROCESSOR HARDWARE CHARACTERISTICS

This section presents some further system details on hardware implementation of architectural design concepts described in the previous section. The operational capability of this hardware, particularly data access times and clock periods, reflects how well the electronic design realizes the signal communication speeds possible with currently used physical principles. The first four sections cover each system in turn. Operational characteristics of the systems are compared so far as possible for similar features of capability in the last section. These comparisons reflect the combined influence of electronic design and central processing unit architecture.

CRAY-1S

The CRAY-1S computer series, introduced in November 1979, has replaced the CRAY-1 computer first marketed in 1976 and represents an evolution of the CRAY-1 product line. Major differences between the CRAY-1 and CRAY-1S are [Auerbach 1981a-g]:

- The CRAY-1S uses a 4-kilobit bipolar memory chip in place of the 1-kilobit chip used on the CRAY-1. Memory capacity has been increased from 1 to 4 megawords.
- The CRAY-1S has enhanced input/output (I/O) architecture capabilities. The CRAY-1S uses a dedicated I/O processor where the CRAY-1 CPU provided direct control of the I/O channels. These capabilities include dedicated disk controllers for each disk drive and IBM channel compatibility. The CRAY-1S can support up to 12 simultaneous disk transfers instead of the four attributed to the CRAY-1. In addition, it has IBM-compatible block multiplexor channels, which may be configured for IBM-compatible peripherals, such as 6250-bpi magnetic tape drives and removable disk drives. The CRAY-1S offers CDC double-density 819 disk drive—600 megabytes in place of 300-megabyte 819 drives on the CRAY-1.

The CRAY-1S series includes 12 models. The primary differences among these models are in the number of I/O processors and memory size. These CRAY-1S models may have up to four I/O processors and 1–4 megawords (64 bits each) of main memory. Models with I/O processors use a buffer memory to buffer I/O transfers. This memory may be 0.5 or 1 megaword. Each I/O processor has a different function:

1. The master I/O processor (MIOP) is used as an operation console and as an interface between the CRAY-1S and 1–3 front-end computers.
2. The buffer I/O processor (BIOP) provides a high-speed channel between the I/O processors and CRAY-1S, and can be used to support disk drives.
3. The block-multiplexor I/O processor (XIOP) is used to support IBM-compatible multiplexor channels.
4. The disk drive I/O processor (DIOP) is used to support double-density CDC 819 disk drives.

Major characteristics of the CRAY-1S CPU are:

- 64-bit word;
- 12.5-nsec clock period;
- scalar and vector processing modes;
- 12 segmented functional units;
- eight 24-bit address primary registers;
- 64 intermediate address registers (24 bits each);
- eight 64-bit scalar primary registers;
- 64 intermediate registers (64 bits each); and
- eight 64-element vector primary registers (64 bits per element).

There are 12 functional units allocated into four groups: address, scalar, vector and floating point. Each functional unit is pipelined into single clock segments, i.e., a result is made available for processing within one clock period.

Primary registers are accessed directly by the functional units. Intermediate registers act as buffers between the primary registers and memory. Address registers are used for memory reference, as index registers, to count loops and to provide shift counts. Scalar registers can contribute one operand to a vector operation or can be loaded from the vector registers, but are used primarily for scalar fixed- and floating-point arithmetic. Vectors are stored and processed by the vector registers. Since vector registers can contain 64 elements, vectors stored within the registers can be of variable length up to 64 elements. Vectors with more than 64 elements are processed in 64-element segments. All eight vector registers may be used concurrently.

The CRAY-1S is primarily used as an additional computational resource to an existing system configuration, not as an independent system. Front-end computers provide the necessary data processing support. The CRAY-1S currently provides hardware interfaces to the following front-end computers:

- CDC CYBER 70/170/700 and 6000/7000,
- IBM 370/3031, and
- Amdahl 470 series.

In addition, future hardware interface capability for the following computers is under development. Model types have not been specified.

- Honeywell,
- Digital Equipment,
- Data General,
- Systems Engineering Laboratories,
- Fujitsu,
- Siemens, and
- Univac.

Local area networking is provided by Network Systems Corporation hyperchannel to interface the CRAY-1S to a local computer network.

Software support for the CRAY-1S includes a multiprogramming batch operating system, two language compilers, diagnostic programs and utilities, as follows:

- COS: CRAY-1S operating system (multiprogramming batch operating system);
- CFT: CRAY FORTRAN IV (FORTRAN 77 compatible);
- CAL: CRAY assembler language;
- UPDATE: scalar language modification system;
- BLAS: basic linear algebra subprograms; and
- CFFT: CRAY fast Fourier transform software.

CDC CYBER 200 Model 205

The CYBER 200 Model 205 represents CDC's most recent effort in developing large-scale high-performance computers. This effort began with the development of the CDC STAR-100 in the early 1970s. Since then, design and implementation of enhancements to the STAR-100 have been based on LSI technology and a bipolar semiconductor memory. These enhancements led to the CYBER 200 series. The first member was CYBER 200 Model 203. This machine featured a high-performance scalar processing unit using LSI technology, a bipolar semiconductor memory of 0.5–2 million 64-bit words, and a vector processing unit using medium-scale integrated (MSI) circuitry.

The present CYBER 200 Model 205 uses LSI technology throughout, featuring a new LSI vector unit integrated with the Model 203 LSI scalar processing unit. The basic version consists of the CPU, 1 million 64-bit words of central memory, eight input/output ports and a maintenance control unit (MCU). The CPU contains the scalar processor and a vector processor with one vector pipeline. Central memory is expandable to 2–4 megawords of memory. Vector pipelines may be expanded to two or four, and the number of I/O ports may be expanded to 16.

The CYBER 205 scalar and vector processors can perform sequential and parallel operations on single bits, 8-bit bytes, and 32- or 64-bit floating point operands and vector elements. The central memory of the CYBER 205 is a high-performance semiconductor memory and provides extremely high storage integrity with single-error correction, double-error detection (SECDED) on each 32-bit halfword. Virtual addressing is employed. Prominent CPU characteristics for the CYBER 205 are (Auerbach 1981a-g]:

- 20-nsec clock period;
- one, two or four parallel vector pipelines;
- independent scalar and vector instruction execution;
- 32- and 64-bit floating point arithmetic;
- vector and sparse vector instructions;
- vector macros;
- dot product instruction; and
- square-root instruction.

The scalar processor also features multiple segmented functional units, which are pipelined to accept new operands every clock cycle. The vector processor can operate in parallel with the scalar processor. Each operand in a vector operation can contain data in sets of up to 65,535 elements (64-bit words).

Vector processing can be performed on 32-bit halfwords as well as 64-bit words. For 32-bit computation, up to 800 million results per second are produced in a four-pipe system. For 64-bit precision, up to 400 million results per second may be produced.

Software support for the Model 205 includes:

- CYBER 200-OS: operating system that provides remote batch and interactive capabilities as well as front-end interface;
- CYBER 200 FORTRAN IV ANSI 77;
- CYBER 200 assembler (META); and
- applications packages, including programs for structural analysis, nuclear reactor safety, weather, seismic data and reservoir simulation.

Like the CRAY-1S, the CYBER 205 is marketed as an additional computational resource and not as a stand-alone system. The software that interfaces the CYBER 205 to a front-end computer system is called Remote Host Facility (RHF). A front-end system such as the CYBER 170 under control of the Network Operating System (NOS) includes RHF software [CDC 1980]. The full set of standard software products on both systems are available to the user. Other front-end computer systems include the CDC 6000 and IBM 370 series. Sperry Univac front-end compatibility is currently under development.

Denelcor HEP

The Denelcor HEP is a large-scale 64-bit computer system whose architecture is MIMD. As such, it is the only commercially available computer of this type. The first HEP was scheduled for delivery in early 1982. The HEP computer consists of PEM, data memory modules and support processors interconnected by a high-speed data switch network. All data memory is accessible by all PEM. Processes executing in parallel in one or more PEM may interact through data sharing. In the HEP, creation and termination of parallel processes are carried out in 100 nsec. These processes are created at any point in the program where parallelism is required. The design of a parallel program is not affected by whether it runs one or several PEM; thus, software modules may be distributed across several PEM. Programs are protected from each other by relocation/protection registers in each PEM. Multiprogramming is thus achieved in the HEP with full user isolation and no operating system intervention.

All data and instruction words in HEP are 64 bits in length. PEM data memory reference instructions allow partial word/byte addressing. The memory bandwidth is 10 megawords/sec per PEM to include data switch network. Each PEM executes up to 10 million scalar or vector instructions per second and can have up to one million words of program memory. In its maximum configuration, 16 PEM may share up to 128 megawords of data memory, yielding an execution rate of 160 million instructions per second.

HEP systems may include high-speed real-time I/O devices connected to the data switch network. An I/O channel interface of 80 megabytes/sec is provided. Normal I/O devices are connected through front-end processors. Available HEP software includes:

- a batch operating system,
- HEP FORTRAN (extended FORTRAN IV, ANSI 66),
- HEP assembler language, and
- HEP Interactive Maintenance Language (IML).

HEP FORTRAN provides explicit parallel programming operations to the programmer. Later versions of HEP FORTRAN will provide automatic parallelism [Auerbach 1981a-g].

Amdahl 580

Slated for market arrival in April 1982, the Amdahl 580 series initially consists of two models—5860 uniprocessor and the 5880 dual-processor configuration. The Amdahl 5860 and 5880 are respectively rated at 2 and 3.5 times the average processing power of the Amdahl 470V/8 [Auerbach 1981a-g]. A key design feature is its compatibility with large-scale IBM systems and with the Amdahl 470 series. As previously discussed, the Amdahl 580 is categorized as conventional SISD architecture. This processor currently represents the most powerful conventional alternative to the vector/parallel processor. The Amdahl 5860 and 5880 have instruction execution rates of 14 and 24 million instructions per second. Prominent features of these are:

- 4-byte word length,
- firmware,
- prefetch pipeline—one instruction/cycle,
- 24-nsec machine cycle time,
- up to 34 I/O channels,
- up to 2 I/O processors, and
- cache storage.

Cache storage of 64 kilobytes is composed of 32 kilobytes each in an instruction buffer (I-buffer) and an operand buffer (O-buffer). A storage unit (S-unit) controls storage and retrieval from memory. The high-speed and main memories are interfaced through the S-unit along with data buses linking the CPU and other 580 series system units.

The 5860 memory is limited to 32 megabytes. The 5880 will include 64 megabytes of main memory and 68 I/O channels as opposed to 32 channels in the 5860.

Amdahl 470 series and IBM system/370 operating systems, including MVS/SP Releases 1, 2 and 3, VM/SP Release 1, and ACP are supported on the 580 series. Developed software can usually run without modification.

Processor Characteristics Compared

Tables 5-1 and 5-2 illustrate performance comparisons of computations in the vector mode for the CDC CYBER 200 Model 205 and the CRAY-1 conducted on a benchmark program at Los Alamos National Laboratory [Bucher and Moore 1981]. The standard unit of measurement is millions of floating point operations per second (MFLOPS). MFLOPS are commonly used to describe performance of vector processors (SIMD) while millions of instructions per second (MIPS) describe performance of SISD machines.

For each computational operation, one million operations were timed for vectors of different lengths. These timing studies were performed on

Table 5-1. CRAY-1 Vector Operation Rates (MFLOPS) for Vectors Stored in Consecutive Locations [Bucher and Moore 1981]

	Vector Length									
Operations[a]	10	25	50	100	200	500	1,000	5,000	10,000	50,000
V = V + S	6.72	13.15	20.20	25.00	27.63	31.95	32.95	33.81	33.99	34.11
V = S × V	6.78	13.61	20.30	25.00	27.54	31.79	32.76	33.60	33.76	33.88
V = V + V	6.11	11.43	16.00	18.78	10.18	22.45	22.92	23.33	23.42	23.47
V = V × V	6.11	11.43	16.00	18.73	20.10	22.36	22.82	23.23	23.31	23.36
V = V + S × V	11.11	19.70	26.40	30.25	32.06	35.01	35.61	36.12	36.23	36.29
V = V × V + S	11.19	21.39	30.53	35.79	38.46	43.08	43.99	44.80	44.97	45.08
V = V × V + V	10.19	17.32	22.47	25.16	26.38	28.41	28.80	29.13	29.20	29.24
V = S × V + S × V	16.67	31.91	45.63	53.57	57.48	64.58	65.97	67.18	67.45	67.62
V = V × V + V × V	14.20	25.00	32.88	36.47	38.06	41.15	41.67	42.12	42.23	42.30

[a] V = vector; S = scalar.

Table 5-2. CYBER 205 Vector Operation Rates (MFLOPS) for Vectors Stored in Consecutive Locations [Bucher and Moore 1981]

	Vector Length									
Operations[a]	10	25	50	100	200	500	1,000	5,000	10,000	50,000
V = V + S	8.93	19.53	32.89	50.00	67.57	83.33	91.24	98.04	99.01	99.80
V = S × V	9.26	20.16	33.78	50.00	68.49	83.33	91.58	98.14	99.01	99.80
V = V + V	8.98	19.53	32.89	50.00	67.57	83.26	91.24	98.04	99.01	99.80
V = V × V	9.26	20.16	33.78	50.00	68.49	83.33	91.58	98.14	99.01	99.80
V = V + S × V	11.90	27.17	48.07	78.09	112.30	152.32	172.86	193.80	196.85	199.20
V = V × V + S	11.90	27.17	48.07	78.09	112.30	152.32	172.86	193.80	196.85	199.20
V = V × V + V	9.26	20.16	33.78	49.99	67.54	83.30	91.09	98.09	99.01	99.80
V = S × V + S × V	10.42	22.86	41.66	63.55	91.44	119.38	132.92	146.20	148.00	148.66
V = V × V + V × V	9.15	19.95	33.48	50.67	66.95	83.68	91.44	98.04	99.04	99.73

[a] V = vector; S = scalar.

Table 5-3. CYBER 203 and CRAY-1 Scalar Operation Rates (MFLOPS) for Operands Stored in Consecutive Locations (Vector Length N = 50,000) [Bucher and Moore 1981]

	CYBER 203, BENCHFTN Compiler		CRAY-1, CFT, Version 1.08	
Operation[a]	Not Optimized	Optimized	Not Optimized	Optimized
V = V + S	1.47	3.12	2.29	2.86
V = V × S	1.47	3.12	2.22	2.76
V = V + V	1.43	2.94	2.16	2.67
V = V × V	1.43	2.94	2.10	2.57
V = V + S × V	2.00	5.55	3.40	4.57
V = V × V + S	2.50	5.88	3.64	4.32
V = V × V + V	1.96	5.26	3.27	4.32
V = S × V + S × V	2.73	7.89	4.44	6.45
V = V × V + V × V	2.63	2.89	4.14	5.85

[a] V = vector; S = scalar.

data stored in consecutive memory locations. A performance comparison of these computational operations performed in a scalar mode is given in Table 5-3. These timing studies were performed using vectors of length N = 50,000. A CYBER 200 Model 203 was used in these timing studies. The CYBER 200 Model 203 has a scalar unit identical to that of the Model 205. It is important to remember that the results depended strongly on the compiler version and degree of optimization.

Performance comparisons on benchmark programs for the Denelcor HEP and Amdahl 580 are still unavailable due to their late arrival in the marketplace. First deliveries for the Amdahl 580 and the Denelcor HEP occurred in early 1982.

All four computers are compared in similar operational features in Tables 5-4 through 5-11. The apparent computational speed advantage of CYBER 205 over CRAY-1S shown in Tables 5-4 and 5-5 has been verified in some of the results of Bucher and Moore [1981]. However, they cite major drawbacks of the CYBER 205 in its inability to access vector elements placed noncontiguously in memory and the longer cycle time (clock period). They found the CRAY compiler better at vectorization, which was a strong factor in their programs. Their final conclusion is that the CRAY-1S would operate slightly faster than the CYBER 205 in most of the codes in the Los Alamos high-speed computer workload.

Table 5-4. CPU Organization

	CYBER 205	CRAY-1S	Denelcor HEP	Amdahl 580
Instruction Word Length(s) (bits)	32 or 64	16 or 32	64	32
Clock Period (nsec)	20	12.5	25	24
Programmable Addressable Registers	256 64-bit	72 24-bit 584 64-bit	2048 64-bit	14 32-bit
Pipeline Segments	Up to 26	Up to 14	Up to 56	5
Max. Vector Results Rate (nsec)	10 (2 pipes) or 5 (4 pipes)	12.5	100 per PEM	Not applicable
Functional (e.g., Arithmetic) Units	14-6 vector, 2 floating point, 1 string, 5 scalar: ADD/SUBM MULT, LOG, SHIFT, DIV, SQRT	12-3 vector, 3 floating point, 2 address, 4 scalar: ADD, SHIFT, LOG, POP/LEAD ZERO count	7 per PEM	4 scalar
Instruction Stack	64 words	64 words	Not applicable	4 half words

Table 5-5. CPU Computation Rates (10^6 computations/sec)[a]

	CYBER 205	CRAY-1S	Denelcor HEP
32-Bit Operands			
Addition	200	80	NA[b]
Multiplication	200	80	NA
Division	25	25	NA
Square Root	25	NA	NA
64-Bit Operands			
Addition	100	80	10[c]
Multiplication	100	80	10[c]
Division	12.5	25	4.7[c]
Square Root	12.5	NA	NA

[a] Data on the Amdahl 580 are still considered proprietary.
[b] NA = not applicable.
[c] Per PEM.

Table 5-6. Central Memory Characteristics

	CYBER 205	CRAY-1S	Denelcor HEP	Amdahl 580
Memory Cycle Time (nsec)	80	50	50	24
Memory Word Length	64 bits (+7 bits SECDED/32 bit half word)	64 bits (+8 bits SECDED)	64 bits (+8 bits SECDED)	32 bits ECC[a] on 8 byte basis
Max. Bandwidth (megawords/sec)	400	320	10/PEM	41
Address Field (bits)	48	24	32	31
Max. Virtual Capacity (megawords)	4×10^{12}	16	147	8
Max. Hardware Capacity (megawords)	4	4	147	8
Standard Working Capacity (megawords)	1	1	0.312	4

[a]ECC = error checking and correction.

Table 5-7. I/O Configuration

	CYBER 205	CRAY-1S	Denelcor HEP	Amdahl 580
Front-End Processor	CYBER 1701, IBM 3031	IBM, CDC, UNIVAC, others	None	Amdahl, IBM
Major Subsystems	Station (control unit and buffer)	I/O subsystem device controller	I/O control, I/O cache system performance instrument	Cache storage instruction pipeline
Processor Word (bits)	16	16	64	32
Memory Cycle Time (nsec)	320	50	50	24
Max. Transfer Rate for STD Channel (megabits/sec)	50	50	20	1.6
Max. Transfer Rate on Direct Access (megabits/sec)	800	850	640	400
Max. Configuration of Channels/Port	16	40	124	34

Table 5-8. Peripheral Characteristics

	CYBER 205	CRAY-1S	Denelcor HEP	Amdahl 580
Disk/Memory Unit	CDC 819-21	CDC 819-21	Ampex DM 9300	IBM 3380
Capacity (megabytes)	600	600	600	600
Access Time (msec)	50	50	28	16
Transfer Rate (megabits/sec)	38.7	38.7	9.6	24
No. Units	Up to 8 drives per controller, up to 10 controllers	Up to 8 drives per controller, up to 32 controllers	31 drives per I/O cache, up to 4 I/O caches	Up to 8 drives per controller, up to 32 controllers
Front-End Processor	CYBER 170-750	IBM, UNIVAC, CDC, others	Not applicable	IBM, Amdahl
Magnetic Tape	Model 679-7	Model 3420, Mod 8	STC 3800	IBM 3420
Density (bpi)	1600/6250	1600/6250	800/1600/6250	1600/6250
Speed (ips)	Up to 200	Up to 200	Up to 125	Up to 200
Transfer Rate (megabytes/sec)	1.5	1.25	0.78	0.78
Record Method	PE/GCR	PE/GCR	PE/GCR	PE/GCR
Line Printer	Not applicable	Not applicable	Documentation impact 1400	IBM 3211
Speed/lpm			900	2000
Chars/line			132	132

Table 5-9. Operating System Characteristics

	CYBER 205	CRAY-1S	Denelcor HEP	Amdahl 580
Main Memory Required (kilowords)	64	48	48	Unavailable
User Interface	JCL, special monitor	JCL, monitor, macro, library	JCL	JCL
Job Switchover Response Time (μsec)	3	5.125	None	Unavailable
Reentrant System Routines/Compilers	Yes/Yes	Yes/No	Yes/Yes	Yes/Yes

Table 5-10. Physical Hardware Characteristics

	CYBER 205	CRAY-1S	Denelcor HEP	Amdahl 580
W × D × H (ft)	18 × 27.5 × 6 (1 megaword)	8.8 diameter × 6.5 height (4 megawords)	9.7 × 4.8 × 6.2, 1 PEM (1 megaword)	12 × 3 × 6 (4 megawords)
Weight (tons)	8 (1 megaword)	5.25 (1 megaword)	6.5 (1 megaword)	4 (4 megawords)
Cooling Req.	Freon/water	Freon/water	Air	Air
High-Density Logic	LSI	SSI	MSI	LSI
Plug in Modules	1760	115	100 per PEM	2
PC Cards	15 layers	5 layers	6 layers	12 layers
Logic	ECL	ECL 1 nsec/gate delay	ECL 3 nsec/gate delay	ECL 400 psec/gate delay

Table 5-11. FORTRAN IV Compiler Characteristics/Features

	CYBER 205	CRAY-1S	Denelcor HEP	Amdahl 580
Standard Compatibility	ANSI 77	ANSI 77	ANSI 66	ANSI 77
Levels of Optimization	3	2	3	3
Diagnostic Levels	Many	3	2	3
Special I/O Statements	Encode/decode, BUF-IN, BUF-OUT, advise, time step	Encode/decode, BUF-IN, BUF-OUT	None	None
Debug Features	DUMP, SNAP, trace debug breakpoint	DUMP, debug XREF symbol table, flowtrace	DUMP, on line, SNAPSHOT, XREF OBJECT, listing	DUMP, SNAP, XREF, trace
Extension Functions	Vector, arithmetic, vector compare, order; min-max dot product, gather/scatter; automatic vectorization option	Automatic vectorization with override option	BASIC BLOCK OPTIMIZATION (PARALLELIZATION), create, asynchronous, variable	None

CHAPTER 6

EXPERIENCE OF VECTOR PROCESSOR USER ORGANIZATIONS

Vector processor user organizations were queried according to the detailed survey format shown in the appendix. In practice, the format was repetitive in many areas and, for summarizing the responses of each user organization, a somewhat simpler outline is used; however, the main divisions of the survey format are followed. Each of the following organizations is discussed independently according to this outline:

- Lawrence Livermore National Laboratory (LLL);
- National Magnetic Fusion Energy Research Computer Center (NMFECC);
- Los Alamos National Laboratory (LANL);
- Sandia National Laboratory, Livermore, California;
- Sandia National Laboratory, Albuquerque, New Mexico;
- Goddard Laboratory for Atmospheric Sciences (GLAS), National Aeronautics and Space Administration (NASA); and
- Geophysical Fluid Dynamics Laboratory (GFDL), Princeton.

Of these laboratories, the first four selected the Cray Research CRAY-1 or CRAY-1S, have been using them, and were therefore able to respond to almost all parts of the survey. The fifth is in the process of installing the current model (CRAY-S1000). The last two laboratories selected the Control Data Corporation (CDC) CYBER 205, which had not yet been delivered. Hence, they were only able to report the circumstances of computational requirements and evaluation criteria that led to their choice. The Cornell and Brookhaven laboratories, which are in the process of choosing the Denelcor Heterogeneous Element Processor (HEP) were not queried in detail, because this system is at an even earlier stage as to market availability than is the CYBER 205. With respect to other relevant user organizations, it was too difficult to arrange detailed interviews within the time frame of the study. However, a short description of systems and mention of principal areas of anticipated application is provided in a subsequent section for:

- Boeing Computing Service;
- United Computing Service;
- Westinghouse Nuclear Energy Center;
- Cornell University;
- U.S. Air Force North American Defense Command;
- U.S. Air Force Weapons Laboratory;
- Brookhaven National Laboratory; and
- Knolls Atomic Power Laboratory and Bettis Atomic Power Laboratory.

LAWRENCE LIVERMORE LABORATORY

LLL, located in Livermore, California, is managed by the University of California for the U.S. Department of Energy (DOE). It has traditionally been equipped with the fastest available computers for its nuclear energy research and development (R&D). In the late 1960s and 1970s these were the CDC 6600 and 7600. Beginning in 1978 the laboratory began acquiring CRAY computers to carry the bulk of its research computational requirements.

Description of Systems

The laboratory has acquired CRAY computers according to the schedule:

- January 1978: CRAY-1,
- June 1979: CRAY-1S, and
- June 1980: CRAY-1S.

However, it was pointed out that there is no substantial difference among the models except for the main memory originally supplied. All three are now each equipped with 1 megaword of main memory and 4.8 gigabytes of disk storage. This is in terms of the CRAY and CDC word length of 8 bytes. The laboratory intended to acquire in 1982 another CRAY-1S with 2 megawords of memory and 9.6 gigabytes of disk storage. All the computers have been purchased outright. According to LLL estimates of lifetime cost, it is 10 times less expensive to own than rent. There are associated maintenance contracts, but no specified penalties for defaults in performance. The maintenance includes approximately four man-years of Cray Research assistance on initial operations, compiler installation and software adjustments. Judging by their past experience with CDC and earlier computers, they anticipate a useful life of approximately 10 years. In the past, as newly available systems became more powerful, the older systems would be replaced. For each system generation, at least one would be held for 10 years. Recently, they sense a declining rate of improvement in new systems, more so in scalar processing capability than in vector processing.

Types of Current or Anticipated Use

About 15% of the LLL budget in recent years has been spent on the computer center. Most of the computer applications to which the CRAY systems are dedicated consist of modeling physical processes. These span a broad range of specific phenomena related to fusion and fission energy generation. While the large integrated computer systems are clearly capable of handling real-time data processing, they are not normally so used at the LLL center. For LLL experiments, real-time processing is normally done by small computers.

Principal Analytic Applications

Most of the mathematical routines used at LLL are packaged. The investigators wish to avoid the task of developing new algorithms when serviceable routines already exist among the many that have been developed over the years at LLL. Most of these are procedures for solving difference equations derived from differential equations that represent hydrodynamic, chemical and nuclear interactions. Such packages would be difficult to revise to take full advantage of vector processing. In most cases, use of the package is part of a development program that does not lead to a substantial code to be used repetitively. Hence, there is little individual incentive to undertake the revisions. In the future there may be a strong collective interest to revise some of the more widely used subroutines.

Nonanalytic Applications

There is no use foreseen of the CRAY systems for any administrative or other nontechnical computer applications. Remaining capability on the older CDC systems is clearly adequate.

Expected Performance and Criteria of Selection

It was expected that the CRAY systems would average about four times faster than the older CDC 7600 system. This average has been achieved, without extensive algorithm vectorization. However, the variation in speed improvement over all the routines is somewhat surprising; it is estimated roughly at 50–1000% of the average.

For benchmark testing in the course of evaluating candidate systems before selection of the CRAY-1 and the CRAY-1S, the LLL computer division used representative parts of real codes that reflected its customary job mix. This was to obtain some idea of how the computers would perform on a normal work load. The total test package amounted to 20,000 lines of FORTRAN, the primary programming language. Since some of the computer load pertains to classified national security work at LLL, further details of the benchmark tests are not available.

Hardware Specifications

The systems are housed in a separate building adjacent to offices and some of the laboratory facilities. They are currently connected to peripherals and user terminals through what LLL calls the Octopus network.

Processing, Communications and Terminal Network

The processors, or worker computers, consisting of the three CRAY systems, older CDC units and a number of smaller computers, are being linked together by a Network System Corporation (NSC) hyperchannel. No front-end processor is required between the CRAY systems and the hyperchannel. The central memory consists of the CRAY mainframe memories augmented by the disks and other mass storage devices, which are centrally controlled to provide an aggregate of 10^{12} bits of archival storage. The main categories of equipment linked together through the network are as follows:

- worker computers (CRAY-1S, etc.);
- central data storage systems;
- remote job entry terminals;
- terminal concentrator computers;
- high-speed printing and hard-copy graphics; and
- soft-copy graphics and television monitors.

Most of the network, without the hyperchannel, was in place before the first CRAY installation in 1978 and it experienced no change in operating characteristics as a result of installing the CRAY systems.

Unusual Features and Near-Term Plans

There is nothing unusual in the network or peripherals except that there is provision for some direct coupling of computer output to the television monitors. The computer division intends to expand the memory in all categories, and there is great interest in acquiring a CRAY-2 when it is available. There are plans to change from the Octopus network to the use of a broad band bus [Nessett and Watson 1981] network. This would be the hyperchannel large-capacity transmission medium (50 megabit/sec coaxial cable) controlled by adapters interfacing between it, the computer and peripheral hosts in such a way that each host appears to be connected to every other host. Each adapter contains a buffer memory and its own central processing unit (CPU) to ensure that the hosts do not interfere with each other. Collectively, they arbitrate the use of the transmission line and match the speed of the transmission to the input/output (I/O) rate of the host by managing their own buffer memory. Usually, the adapter collects data from the transmission medium at a high rate, stores it temporarily, then retransmits data to the host at a lower rate.

Software

Among computer center staff and the scientific investigators, LLL possesses considerable expertise in programming and the development of computers for high-level languages. Hence, they need not rely heavily on the assistance Cray Research is ready to provide.

High-Level Language Compilers

CRAY compilers have been used, but not exclusively. It is estimated that more use is probably made of LLL's own compilers such as CIVIC. This provides the basic FORTRAN with local extensions beyond what is available in the CRAY FORTRAN compiler. With respect to automatic vectorization, the two compilers are about equal. LLL judged that their optimization produced similar running times within a few percent.

Assembly Languages

There have been no large application programs written in assembly language. Occasionally, very small subroutines that are frequently used may be developed as an optimal assembly language package. The sum total of such lines of code is considered negligible, although it may occupy a substantial part of the running time on the machine.

Operating Systems

Most of the computing jobs are run on a basis of operator-controlled, batch-type, time-sharing. There is little call for interactive use. Large batch jobs are done mostly at night with the operations staff handling them manually. Interactive work is allowed on the system, but only at a high priority level. Most of the jobs require a total execution time of around 5 min.

Special Software Packages

Few special software packages are bought from sources outside LLL. One notable example is the EISPAK set. This consists of numerical mathematics routines for the solution of differential equations, evaluation of functions and statistical integrals. Some proprietary packages in FORTRAN, which are maintained centrally, can be accessed from all the terminals of the network, and are processed through the CRAY FORTRAN compiler.

Significant Advantages

The prime advantage of the CRAY computers is the running time, which averages 25% of that of CDC 7600. There is admittedly a large variation among the programs, but none performed poorly on the CRAY compared to the CDC 7600. Those that did very much better than average had vectorized kernel algorithms.

Only in the first few months of operation were any problems experienced in bringing the system into the existing configuration. However, LLL is accustomed to conversion among large processing systems, and the communications network was designed to accept new CPU, other new devices or new configurations among the existing devices. Generally, programmers experienced little difficulty as long as the programs were in FORTRAN.

There was considerable help available for analytical support from onsite Cray Research analysts. Some of them are still on hand to maintain the CRAY computer and help with related user problems.

During installation there were no delays beyond a day or two. In fact, one of the system deliveries was too early. There were no delays in responding to the few special requests of LLL. However, LLL was not sure of how well Cray Research might respond in the future or with less self-reliant customers. The Cray Research staff is estimated as very small, only 1000 total.

Significant Problem Areas

It is expected to take a few years to take complete advantage of the vector processing feature in the development of new algorithms. Generally, programs were shifted from the CDC 7600 to the CRAY systems without serious trouble. However, the CIVIC compiler, designed for the CDC 7600, posed a more difficult problem. Problems are anticipated over the next 10 years as multiprocessors, to which LLL is not accustomed, are brought into the center. The CRAY-2, when it is available, will be a multiprocessor.

Cray Research seems to be relatively slow to incorporate into its system new developments in hardware or software. LLL in-house systems personnel are used for rapid introduction of new software. There was some increase in the requirements for electric power and cooling water for the computing system itself. However, there is a relatively large increment of power required for the compressors in the Freon cooling fluid loop. In addition, a new 440-V line and other special gear for the electric power system were needed for the compressors. The compressor systems for the Freon coolant are noisy and must be kept in a separate area.

Level of Satisfaction

Unsurpassed operational reliability is a main ingredient of LLL satisfaction with the CRAY systems. They are available 95% of the time. Maintenance and service are adequate. Technical support is adequate. The manufacturer's software may not be adequate for other centers, but LLL uses mostly its own software. Programming to take full advantage of the vector processing feature will be a continuing burden.

General Commentaries

There are no serious limitations or problems for LLL. However, it is possible that other centers would be seriously hampered if Cray Research does not furnish time-sharing software. For a laboratory with many small R&D problems, there is a need for better time-sharing. As described in the next section, a time-sharing system for CRAY computers has been developed by NMFECC. It is being used on their network, at LLL and at LANL. Laboratories with mostly large-scale production programs can better use a purely batch environment.

NATIONAL MAGNETIC FUSION ENERGY COMPUTER CENTER

The laboratories of this facility are located at LLL. However, they are under a separate administration and operate their own computer center wholly dedicated to magnetic fusion energy, which is one of the largest DOE research programs. It is the hub of an extensive network of other facilities engaged in magnetic fusion energy research and using the high-speed processors at the center. This network is shown in Figure 6-1.

Description of Systems

NMFECC has acquired CRAY computers according to the schedule:

- May 1978: CRAY-1, and
- September 1981: CRAY-1S.

These systems are considered identical except for size of main memory originally supplied. The first CRAY system has 1 megaword of main memory and 4.8 gigabytes of disk storage. The second has 2 megawords of main memory and 9.6 gigabytes of disk storage. Although the standard CRAY system must include a front-end processor, such as the CDC 7600, NMFECC does not use it. They have their own executive operating system that enables them to interface with their communication links directly, as is done at LLL.

Anticipated operational lifetime for the CRAY-1 systems is about seven years, judging by the center's past experience. For example, at present, their CDC 7600, acquired in the mid 1970s, handles only 9% of the computational requirement. Probably the CRAY-1S will be superseded by the CRAY-2 sometime before 1985.

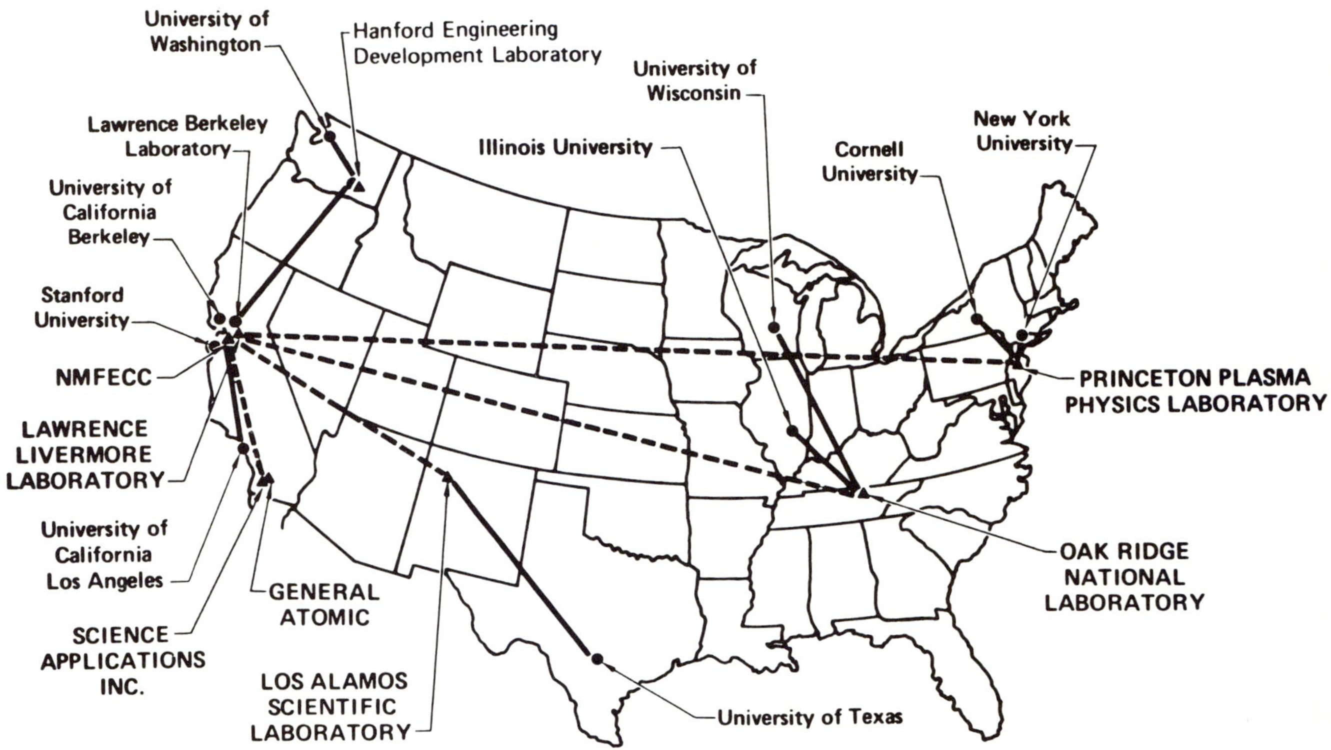

Figure 6-1. National Magnetic Fusion Energy Computer Center (NMFECC) network. - - - = 50-megabit line; ——— = medium-speed line [DOE 1978].

The CRAY-1 was purchased outright by the center. The CRAY-1S was acquired through what is known as a lease/purchase agreement. A bank, as independent party, has agreed to finance the purchase until ownership is achieved by NMFECC through periodic payments. By its terms NMFECC cannot bow out of the contract. Both CRAY systems were bought through competitive procurement that included benchmark trials and acceptance tests. The bank had no voice in the evaluation.

There was a standard maintenance contract that included assistance in initial operations and some software support. This amounted to 3–4 Cray Research analysts for a few years. The center undertook substantial responsibility for the software under provisions that are not in the standard Cray Research contract. Traditionally, NMFECC has sought to "unbundle" software support.

Types of Current or Anticipated Use

The center is almost exclusively dedicated to computations modeling the plasma phenomena of magnetic thermonuclear fusion. There are some studies of safeguards for magnetic fusion reactors and of nonelectric applications of fusion. These last would pertain to synfuels production and involve simulation codes for chemical processes.

Principal Analytical Applications

Most of the programs are developed in-house to represent the physical processes of fusion. These are only used for a short time before being superseded by other programs. As with LLL, the most important mathematical procedures are difference equations to represent the dynamic interactions of particles over large and sometimes irregularly shaped regions. Certain standard algorithms, such as one for a fast Fourier transform (which was developed at NMFECC), have become generally used subroutines. For engineering problems that arise in the course of implementing the large magnetic fusion experiments, NMFECC has developed a large set of application codes. There is little use of outside packaged routines.

Nonanalytic Applications

There are no administrative or other nonanalytic applications of the CRAY systems.

Expected Performance and Criteria of Selection

Under the foregoing circumstances, and without allowing for further improvement after algorithms are vectorized, the center realistically expected from the CRAY systems running times of 25–33% of those experienced on the CDC 7600. They are actually doing somewhat better, with run times of 20–25% of those on the CDC 7600. This is what most investigators at the center had been hoping for. During the procurement process, benchmark tests were run for each system. These consisted primarily of whole codes from each major time-consuming user, with some modification so that they could be run individually. Besides operation time, the evaluation criteria included such aspects as main memory available, peripheral storage arrangements, word size and vectorization problems. For the CRAY-1, there were somewhat easy requirements for compatibility with existing software. The requirements were much more stringent when the CRAY-1S was acquired. In the expected job mix there were really two categories. Around 90% of the jobs are short-time and will occupy about 5% of the total computer time. These are candidates for time-sharing and interactive use. Around 10% of the jobs are large computational types run only in the batch mode, and consume 95% of the time.

Hardware Specifications

The CRAY-1 and CRAY-1S computers are located within the single NMFECC building. As with the CDC computers, they are run on 400-cycle power. Heavy flywheels are installed on their motor generator shafts to maintain power through temporary utility power failures. Backup emergency power is available through battery- and diesel-based systems.

Processing, Communications and Terminal Network

Each of the two CRAY acquisitions was a standard $10 million package. The center uses no printers or card handlers in the immediate physical surroundings of the CRAY systems. The network communication is based on satellite relays and microwave links. The remotely located user service centers (Figure 6-1) usually interface with the main line through PDP 11/40 remote communications control processors. Each center has a PDP-10 KL computer (made by Digital Equipment Corporation) enabling it to function as a remote output or a remote job entry station. They also function as terminal concentrators, linking local hard-wired or dial-up terminal users to the main computers at the center in Livermore, California. The CRAY disk storage proved insufficient for the center's needs. Hence, there are no permanent files on the disks; instead, they are placed on a centrally controlled and automated mass storage, known as MASSTOR, located in nearby Sunnyvale, California. Time-sharing is accomplished at the center using the operating system developed in-house, which is now known as the CRAY Time-Sharing System (CTSS).

Unusual Features and Near-Term Plans

Aside from the rather extensive network of remotely located user service centers, there are no unusual features at the NMFECC facility. Their future plans include the purchase of more CRAY-caliber machines; however, this depends on continued growth of the fusion research community. If future funding continues at current projections, they expect at most one more large machine in the next five years.

Software

While the NMFECC staff possesses programming expertise similar to that of LLL, they have chosen to place more reliance on the assistance and packages Cray Research is ready to provide.

Bilevel Language Compilers

The center depends primarily on the CRAY FORTRAN compiler. However, NMFECC uses its own compilers for utility programs and system operation.

Assembly Languages

Very little assembly-language programming is done. It is only used for a very definite and substantial gain in run time. Generally, the center's directors tend to discourage its use.

Operating Systems

The center uses its own operating system to have both time-sharing and interactive capability on the large number of developmental programming projects.

Special Software Packages

Special packages are rarely used. There is no use of proprietary or classified software. The center has a lot of its own software that has not yet been tested comprehensively on a large data base.

Significant Advantages

The most important advantages of the CRAY computers to the center are their rapid response time and their excellent reliability. They attribute this to the medium-scale integrated (MSI) solid-state technology (4–16 kilobits per chip).

There were no difficulties in reconfiguration and expansion of the NMFECC system to incorporate the new CRAY machinery. The two systems proved to be much simpler to install than the CDC 7600 or CYBER 175 with which they have had experience.

In weighing qualitative costs and benefits, they see little additional cost to the end user. Users must know how to handle the new architecture. Many programs had to be recompiled and the models reformulated for better compatibility with a vector processing system. There were no problems with respect to delivery and installation of hardware or delivery of required software.

Significant Problem Areas

The main problem, which did not matter much to NMFECC, is the lack of time-sharing in the CRAY system software. Hence, the center rejected most of it. Cray Research's developmental pace is somewhat slow and they are reluctant to incorporate new ideas that originated elsewhere. NMFECC estimated twofold increase overall in required electrical power.

Level of Satisfaction

High operational reliability and ease of installation of the CRAY systems were surprising features that NMFECC did not expect. NMFECC is also getting all it expected in improved speed of operation. Maintenance and service are adequate. Technical support is adequate. Software outside of the compilers and assemblers is inadequate. The only programming difficulties experienced by users has been the need to revise programs for the vector processing architecture.

General Commentaries

The CRAY software environment is substantially poorer than that of CDC or IBM. In addition, there is excessive reliance on a front-end processor for the usual installation. Debugging programs could be hampered by the front-end processor hiding real problems.

A lot of code development in the operating system was required and NMFECC seriously considered seeking a different machine to get the interactive capability. For production runs with large numbers of computations, the CRAY-1S should do very well.

LOS ALAMOS NATIONAL LABORATORY

Like LLL, LANL, located in Los Alamos, New Mexico, is managed by the University of California for DOE. Its responsibilities are very similar to those of the combined Livermore complex of LLL and NMFECC. It is one of the main user stations linked to the NMFECC.

Description of Systems

LANL was the earliest DOE laboratory in acquiring CRAY computing systems. Four have been installed according to the schedule:

- March 1976: CRAY-1, upgraded to CRAY-1A with 1 megaword of mainframe memory;
- April 1979: CRAY-1A, upgraded to CRAY-1S in 1980 with 2 megawords of memory;
- April 1981: CRAY-1A, with 1 megaword of main memory; and
- October 1981: CRAY-1S, with 2 megawords of main memory.

The model nomenclature is somewhat inconsistent among the installations. Individual CRAY units all bear a nameplate that reads "CRAY-1." There are no suffix letters. At other installations the "S" means the use of 4K chips instead of 1K in the CPU and mainframe memory. At LANL they are named according to how much mainframe memory is attached as follows:

- CRAY-1: 0.5 megaword,
- CRAY-1A: 1 megaword, and
- CRAY-1S: 2 megawords.

The computer obtained in April 1981 is rented. The other three have all been purchased under five-year lease/purchase agreements similar to that of the NMFECC, so that now the earliest CRAY system has been fully paid for.

Types of Current or Anticipated Use

Most of the LANL Computing Division's work is related to military technology development. The remainder pertains to fusion energy research and current problems in fission reactor operation, safety, waste management, fuel cycle and safeguards. There is also some work associated with new and renewable energy sources, but the DOE budget for this has not been as stable as for nuclear energy work at LANL.

Principal Analytic Applications

One of the major difficulties experienced in optimizing programs to execute on the CRAY system stems from the high proportion of Monte Carlo calculations that are used to obtain statistical results. Efficient operation of a vectorized code is hampered by the lack of special gather/scatter instructions such as those of the CDC CYBER 205. Another problem that was mentioned is that, in simulating plasma phenomena for fusion studies, many of the algorithms use nested subscripts for a function expressed in FORTRAN as: A(I(J)). In this case there does not appear to be any general way to vectorize for the CRAY system.

Some examples in which they have had success in vectorizing were cited by LANL survey response. For table look-up operations, which are very frequent in calculating equations of state, LANL vectorizes by special design of the data structures. With optimal FORTRAN, threefold improvements have been achieved. For recursion relations, commonly used in modeling diffusion [e.g., U(I) = f(U(I − 1))], vectorization is achieved through elliptic difference equation techniques [Buzbee et al. 1977].

LANL focuses its vectorization efforts on relatively large codes that consume hundreds of hours on the CRAY-1. This has produced some significant results. For example, by rewriting about 5000 lines of a hydrodynamics code, an overall ninefold speedup was obtained relative to the CDC 7600.

Many of the application programs at LANL are run on the CRAY computers without revision to optimize for vector processing. They are run in the scalar mode because the investigators do not take time for conversion when they are anxious for immediate results at each stage of their research. A recent Computing Division experiment showed that complete vectorization of existing code for some applications is extremely expensive. For a very large classified code (100,000 lines), a 90% vectorization required 50 man-years of effort.

Nonanalytic Applications

Administrative and other nonanalytic applications are not placed on the CRAY systems. Administrative work is kept on two CDC CYBER 73 units.

Performance Expected and Criteria of Selection

The Computing Division was primarily interested in a substantial improvement in running time with scalar and vector processing capabilities considered of equal importance. They have a standard benchmark library at LANL developed along the ideas described by Bucher and Moore [1981]. Such a library is regarded as essential for their evaluation procedure among the next generation of supercomputers. Because scalar processing occupies so much time in LANL applications, scalar processing capability is considered to be the most important or limiting factor in performance evaluation.

Hardware Specifications

The Computing Division, with its CRAY systems, is located in a wing of the main building at LANL. It services a large number of remote terminals located throughout the complex of experimental buildings at Los Alamos. There is some distributed processing carried out with some of the smaller remotely located systems. In addition, LANL is a user service station in the NMFECC network.

Processing, Communications and Terminal Network

The entire computer network at LANL is known as the Integrated Computer Network (ICN). The CRAY systems play a central role in this network, along with the Computing Division's Common File System (CFS), which is a file management and mass storage system accessible to all of the 3400 users of the ICN. For each CRAY system, there are four disk drives installed and associated disk memory capacity that may be linked through the CRAY system controllers:

1. CRAY-1A (1976): seventeen D819, CDC, 300 megabytes each, maximum = 5.2 gigabytes;
2. CRAY-1S (1980): seventeen D819, CDC, 300 megabytes each, maximum = 5.2 gigabytes;
3. CRAY-1A (1981): eight DD829, CDC, 600 megabytes each, maximum = 4.8 gigabytes; and
4. CRAY-1S (1981): eight DD829, CDC, 600 megabytes each, maximum = 4.8 gigabytes.

In addition to the CRAY systems, there are the following processing units and associated operating systems integrated into the network:

Number	Processor	Operating System
4	CDC 7600	LTSS
1	CDC 6600	NOS
2	CDC CYBER 73 (administrative use only)	NOS
20	DEC VAX 11/780 (distributed data base processing)	VMS

Some of the other peripheral units attached to the network are:

- Common File System (CFS), 4.4 terabits operated with IBM 370/448 and 4341 under VSI, 20 IBM 3350 disk drives, and dual controllers, 2 data paths;
- output station: pages, dual controllers, single paths operated with 2 VAX 11/780;
- microfilm and microfiche III-FR80;
- 2 Versatec plotters; and
- 2 Xerox 9700 printers (10,000 lines per minute).

Unusual Features and Near-Term Plans

In addition to the laboratory work at LANL, the Computing Division also processes work from a few other DOE test sites. To do this the following capabilities have been developed at LANL:

- XNET switches for distributed processing and servicing remote sites;
- terminal pass-through capacity; and
- operating systems for intelligent terminals at test sites.

The division's computer center operations are run continuously, 24 hours per day, and 7 days per week, with a staff of 65 operators and 10 support personnel.

Current plans include an additional CRAY-1S with four megawords of main memory and eight DD 829 disk drives by 1983. By 1985 they expect to add a computer from the next generation (not yet fully defined but probably 3–5 times faster than the CRAY-1S). Optical (laser-based sensing) disk technology is being considered. A satellite link to NMFECC will be established shortly. By 1990, the division expects to be serving 6000 users.

Software

LANL uses commercial and in-house system software. In addition, LANL develops its own protocols for its communication network DECNET, which must also be compatible with the Livermore–developed CTSS.

High-Level Language Compilers

For the majority of user programs, the CRAY FORTRAN Compiler (CFT) has proven sufficiently serviceable. In addition, the Computing Division has developed its own special variant compiler known as CIVIC. It allows a more flexible format for definition of array and vector data structures and calls for vector processing explicitly. Most users are sufficiently sophisticated that they need no substantial education for conversion of their programs.

Assembly Language Conversion Requirements

Very little assembly-language programming is used.

Operating Systems

LANL uses the CTSS developed at the NMFECC to provide time-sharing and interactive capability.

Special Software Packages

At LANL, a selection of utility programs grouped in libraries for specific application categories has been developed to be compatible with the CTSS.

Significant Advantages

The CRAY systems at LANL are valued primarily for their scalar processing capability. It is estimated that at least 15% of any LANL program is inherently scalar. If scalar processing is several times slower than vector processing, at least half the computation time is occupied in scalar processing. As the remainder of the program is more completely optimized for vector processing, the scalar processing speed becomes the limiting factor.

The reliability and availability record being set by four CRAY systems particularly impressed LANL staff. Outside of preventive maintenance (about 3 hours per week), the first CRAY has been available 99% of the time. The remaining CRAY systems average 93–96% availability with combined allocation of 8 hours per week for preventive maintenance.

For the first CRAY system, six months were required for design, preparation and final installation. This period was reduced for subsequent systems, and was down to eight weeks for the most recent one. The CRAY systems also show excellent recovery from utility power failures.

Level of Satisfaction

Reliability and availability are unexpectedly very high. Maintenance and service are adequate. Technical support is adequate. The manufacturer's operating system software was inadequate for LANL needs, but the Computing Division and NMFECC have developed their own, which is very serviceable. Program conversion has not been a problem to LANL users.

General Commentaries

In general the LANL Computing Division staff was highly satisfied with the CRAY systems acquired thus far. However, the staff has the capability to compensate for some very definite deficiencies of Cray Research support, notably the lack of time-sharing in the operating systems Cray offers. The LANL investment in CRAY systems is now fairly large and it would be difficult to convert to a new computer unless a performance improvement factor of four to five is realized. On the other hand, they would be cautious about suggesting the CRAY systems unequivocally to prospective users, especially if they lack the systems expertise of LANL.

SANDIA NATIONAL LABORATORY, LIVERMORE, CALIFORNIA

The Sandia National Laboratory at Livermore, California, is managed by the Western Electric Company of American Telephone and Telegraph for DOE, and is located adjacent to LLL. Its R&D activities are a mixture similar to that of LLL, but the orientation of its research activities is more applied. The anticipated return on its work, in the form of realized practical improvements in energy technology, is expected to be more certain and require less time.

Description of Systems

At Sandia—Livermore, the system consists of a CRAY-1S processor 0.5 megaword of central memory (1 word = 8 bytes) and a CDC 6600 as front-end processor. The CRAY unit was installed in September 1980, following standard U.S. Government Services Administration (GSA) procurement procedures. The purchase contract included a standard hardware maintenance contract worded very much like those for the CDC equipment. The mode of acquisition starts with a leasing arrangement for 30 months, after which the equipment will be purchased outright. Considering the anticipated obsolescence of the CRAY system compared to new developments and the availability of funds for new systems, Sandia—Livermore expects to keep the system running for about eight years.

Types of Current or Anticipated Use

With greater emphasis toward immediately applicable technology development, Sandia—Livermore tends to emphasize nuclear reactor safety, new and renewable energy resources, and environmental studies in their scientific applications of the computer. Most programs are developed in-house; about 5% are packages purchased from other organizations. The computing center is run as an open shop with several hundred scientific users. Heavy production work occurs only in structural analysis and heat dynamics. There is no strong drive toward vectorizing programs for the CRAY system. Most investigators rely on the vectorizing capability of the CRAY FORTRAN compiler.

Principal Analytic Applications

The range of technical problems treated is surprisingly broad, but the solution of linear systems of differential equations generally is the main work. For example, the following specific subjects were cited to illustrate the nature of the scientific work being carried on at Sandia—Livermore.

- fission reactors: Monte Carlo calculation of neutron damage to reactor vessel material using 1000-atom lattice samples;
- renewable energy: Monte Carlo calculations of the influence on central solar receiver mirror fields of a variety of causes of lost radiation, such as shadowing, blocking, tracking errors and atmospheric attenuation;
- combustion: generation of pollutants by fossil fuel burning, experimental laser diagnostic technique using scattered light interrogation of the combustion zone, and comparison with simulation of chemical kinetics involving 100 or more possible reactors; and
- defects in solids: calculation of electronic wave functions for interaction energy of helium or hydrogen atoms placed in interstitial positions.

Nonanalytic Applications

There are no administrative or other nonanalytic applications of the CDC 6600 and CRAY-1S system.

Expected Performance and Criteria of Selection

Sandia—Livermore began the procurement process after the first LLL CRAY-1 system had been operating several years. Hence, they expected a similar level of performance improvement, hopefully 3–5 times better execution speed on their own mix of programs. They found that their codes, previously written for the CDC 6600, when converted on the CRAY compiler, ran 8–9 times faster on average, some up to 20 times; however, some exhibited only a 50% improvement. The Monte Carlo codes, of which they use many, did not do so well because of the large number of branching statements. The gather-scatter operation required for vectorization proved very expensive in execution time. A great benefit, which they had not expected, was the speed of the compiler. They felt that it was running 40 times as fast as the CDC compiler for the 6600.

As part of the procurement process, the competing systems were tested on three sets of benchmark programs. Set 1 was a single FORTRAN program, SPEED, designed to measure the speed of the CPU and determine if the system met the minimum performance standard specified in the GSA request for quotation. The program contained five kernels chosen from codes that had already been run frequently on the CDC 6600 and modified so that they could be run easily. Set 2 was a collection of eight complete production codes already part of the Sandia—Livermore workload. The competing vendors were allowed to change the codes so that the same number of floating point operations would be executed. Set 3 was a group of 100 small FORTRAN programs to test the features and speed of the compiler. These programs, which contained some errors, were not sent to the vendors before the benchmark testing so as to learn how the vendor's programmers would treat unanticipated problems.

Primary criteria for the whole test were execution time, memory provision and compiler operation. In addition, following standard GSA guidelines, Sandia—Livermore required 90% availability at rated performance, a hardware maintenance contract similar to the CDC standard and two analysts onsite. There was some flexibility in this last requirement. A total level of about 48 man-months of support from Cray Research is expected.

Hardware Specifications

The main systems are placed in an underground facility. This has made for some ease in controlling ambient temperature, although that is not considered significant. Of greater importance is the ease with which the facility can be kept secure.

Processing, Communications and Terminal Network

The system is relatively small and simple compared to those described in the previous sections. The CPU consists of the CDC 6600 front-end processor, the CRAY-1S main processor and the 0.5 megaword of main memory. Main data storage is on eight DD 829 disk units, which provide up to 4.8 gigabytes of storage. Printers and card readers are accessed through the CDC 6600. There are three remote job entry terminals and a large number of Tectronix 4014 interactive graphics terminals.

Unusual Features and Near-Term Plans

The computer group is interested in extending the use of the interactive graphics equipment and they intend to add new models of the terminals as they become available. The central memory limit of 0.5 megaword is considered a severe handicap and it is expected that the memory will be increased to at least 1 megaword.

Software

Compared to the laboratories in previous sections, Sandia—Livermore has a relatively small staff: 6–7 systems programmers. Hence, there is a tendency to use whatever software CRAY has available.

High-Level and Assembly Language Compilers

The staff places almost exclusive reliance on the CRAY compilers. In some cases they have been able to buy them as a standard product. There is some concern about optimizing the object code for faster execution. However, without the staff or user time available, they tend to seek other ways to resolve such programming issues.

Some important features of the CRAY FORTRAN compiler are as follows: it provides indications of which loops have been vectorized and what other loops can possibly cause problems. There are additional messages stating why certain loops were not vectorized. Also, indications as to how the execution time was used among the loops show which loops are the most important to vectorize. Pursuing this technique usually gives twofold improvement in speed. The compiler itself is so fast because full use of the vector capability has been included in its design. The Sandia—Livermore staff has found that they need not bother with any recompilation of part of a program since the entire program can be done so quickly. This feature has been very useful in building a library of their own programs.

Operating System

The CDC 6600 operates a network type arrangement using the CDC supplied NOS/BE in a batch environment. The CRAY-1S is operated under the CRAY Operating System (COS) and in fact the Sandia—Livermore system was used as the test site for the last operating version of the COS. The operating system, however, is still young, and there are many desirable features that the Sandia—Livermore staff thinks should be incorporated.

Significant Advantages

Besides the great improvement in program execution speed, stressed as the most important benefit by users, there has also been the very fast FORTRAN compiler time. From the standpoint of a user who is almost always developing a new program rather than running an already perfected program, this feature means much more in terms of facilitating his overall research effort. Compilation time in the developmental stages of programming can normally be much greater than running time. With the CRAY compiler, it becomes negligible and essentially their available computation time is at least doubled. The systems programmers add that the CRAY seems to be extremely reliable with availability in a typical month being greater than 95%.

Significant Problem Areas

No significant problem areas were associated with installing the system hardware and converting the existing CDC 6600 programs to run on the CRAY. Differing with some of the other respondents, the Sandia—Livermore staff did not experience any effect on system operations of changes in either the hardware or software for the CRAY-1S. The changes were evolutionary and occurred about every six months. Usually they would be small revisions of the operating system. It was pointed out that because Cray Research used the Sandia—Livermore system as a test site, they tended to get extra help from them. Some users were a little disappointed that Cray Research provides so little in applications programs.

The only problem Sandia—Livermore staff could mention—it was considered very minor—is the noise from the operation of the auxiliary equipment to compress and circulate the Freon coolant. This was placed in a separate isolated basement room so that any noise in the main computer room was masked by the noise of the air conditioning equipment and disk drives. Over the entire working history of the unit, until now, there has been only one compressor failure. In all it was found that about twice the power and cooling is required for the CRAY-1S as for the CDC 6600.

Level of Satisfaction

Ease of operation was considered exceptional. There were some minor difficulties in converting the programs, but since the system was available

Table 6-1. Sandia—Livermore Computing Center Production Summary

	Machine	Unscheduled Downtime (%)	MTBF[a] (hr)	MTTR[b] (hr)	Total Downtime (%)	MUP[c] (hr)	MDN[d] (hr)
June 21– July 20	6600A	1.3	64.6	0.9	4.5	62.5	3.2
	6600B	1.7	44.2	0.8	6.1	42.2	2.9
	Cray	6.9	95.7	8.3	14.1	88.2	17.1
July 21– August 20	6600A	0.8	69.2	0.6	2.9	67.8	2.2
	6600B	3.7	56.9	2.3	4.9	56.2	3.2
	Cray	0.8	38.1	0.3	4.5	36.7	1.8
August 21– September 20	6600A	0.8	108.8	1.0	3.7	105.6	4.8
	6600B	3.7	49.3	2.0	9.0	46.8	4.7
	Cray	0.8	126.9	1.3	5.0	121.2	8.2
	VAX	2.0	156.8	4.9	5.0	152.1	11.8

[a] MTBF = mean time between failures.
[b] MTTR = mean time to repair.
[c] MUP = month uptime.
[d] MDN = month downtime.

to running codes within a week of installation, it was not considered serious.

The mainframe is considered extremely reliable. To illustrate this, Table 6-1 compares downtime on the CRAY with that on some of the other systems run by the Sandia—Livermore computing center.

The same Cray Research group services LLL and Sandia—Livermore with office and storage space provided. Typically, they respond within 10 min for any trouble and down time is rarely more than 20 min.

Technical support has been adequate. A training program was written into the contract for 10 operators, 10 systems programmers, some applications programming and a joint Sandia-Cray Research analytic effort. The documentation is adequate but not as complete or voluminous as that of IBM. Otherwise, it is better than most and certainly superior to the CDC documentation.

The manufacturer's software is uneven. There is not much in the way of applications programs, but the FORTRAN compiler is very satisfactory. Program conversion has so far not proved troublesome because of the compiler features.

General Commentaries

Without question, the CRAY-1S is accomplishing what it was supposed to do for Sandia—Livermore. The most serious problems anticipated are in training the general users to rewrite their codes and in interfacing with a front-end processor. There is some lack of interface capability with many types of machines. In addition, due to insufficient buffer memory space, only one front-end processor can be coupled to the CRAY-1S.

The main recommendation to be passed on to a prospective user is to avoid starting with only 0.5 megaword of main memory. It is much better to have at least 1 megaword.

SANDIA NATIONAL LABORATORY, ALBUQUERQUE, NEW MEXICO

The Sandia facility at Albuquerque has essentially the same R&D responsibilities relative to LANL (50 miles away) as has the Sandia—Livermore Laboratory relative to LLL. Sandia—Albuquerque is relatively late in acquiring a vector processor computer so that there is very little experience to report. However, information was provided on the rationale and expectations that underlie its acquisition.

Description of Systems

At Sandia—Albuquerque, a CRAY-S1000 with 1 megaword of main memory was tentatively scheduled for delivery in January 1982. The purchase contract allows 90 days of leeway so that at best the new installation is still in the initial trial stages. As with Sandia—Livermore, GSA procedures were followed for a lease with option to purchase. The CRAY system will be integrated into the present system by having a CDC 6613 serve as front-end processor. The expected operational life of the new system is seven years.

Types of Current or Anticipated Use

Differing slightly from Sandia—Livermore, Sandia—Albuquerque tends to emphasize nuclear reactor safety, nuclear waste disposal and alternative energy resources in their scientific applications of the computer. As part of laboratory effort in alternative energy resources, Sandia—Albuquerque is building the electron beam fusion accelerator EBFA-1. Hence, a substantial computer application in inertial confinement fusion must also be included. There is likely to be a somewhat lower proportion of programs developed in-house than at Sandia—Livermore. At Sandia—Albuquerque, more use will be made of programs that have been developed elsewhere by DOE and its laboratories and by the Nuclear Regulatory Commission (NRC) for special purposes.

Principal Analytic Applications

The following categories of analysis were cited as areas of applications that the users were most anxious to place on the CRAY system:

- RELAP series: codes developed under NRC sponsorship to simulate severe accidents during which drastic departures from nominal operating conditions will occur;
- fault tree analysis: simulation of accident consequences according to probabilities of specific failures leading to different chains of events according to the arguments originally presented in the Rasmussen report on reactor safety [NRC 1975]; and
- shock wave propagation: numerical simulation of explosive fracturing for the oil shale retorting process, currently hampered in the fidelity of their operation by the coarse mesh that must be used to limit the CDC 6613 execution time.

Nonanalytic Applications

No administrative or other nonanalytic applications will be part of the workload of the CRAY-S1000.

Expected Performance and Criteria of Selection

As stated in the computer acquisition justification statement submitted by Sandia—Albuquerque [Sandia 1979], the first requirement for the computer was capability to perform at least 20 million floating point operations per second (MFLOPS) on typical FORTRAN programs with only modest modifications and with "single precision" of at least 10 decimal digits. Next, the central memory had to be at least 1 million words, and finally, the disk (or other bulk) memory must have a minimum capacity of 20 billion bits (2.5 gigabytes).

Tests were made of unmodified programs run in the scalar mode with no explicit vectorization. The systems programmers at Sandia—Albuquerque expect to eventually convert some of the assembly language routines of the older codes. Three kinds of programs were run for the tests:

- unmodified production codes;
- general library functions (generic routines); and
- codes requiring a large amount of data handled through the I/O interface.

Some important provisions for integration of the processor into the existing system were:

- A CDC 6613 under NOS would serve as the front-end processor.
- The vendor would provide both hardware and software interfaces for the front-end processor.
- The vendor would provide networking software compatible with the existing network.
- The vendor would demonstrate software.

There was no specific performance requirement on the front-end processor. The overall decision formula was expressed in FORTRAN notation as:

```
SS = LTDS*0.250 + TPS*0.450 + CPS*0.300
```

where SS = selection score
LTDS = line test demonstration score
TPS = technical performance score
CPS = cost performance score

The last three scores represent a comparison among the competitors with each judged on a scale of 0 to 1. Hence, the scale of the selection score is also from 0 to 1.

The software requirements primarily concerned the FORTRAN compiler, which had to be compatible with FORTRAN 66, and the following special features:

- Vectorization must be automatic.
- There must be diagnostic tools for program optimization.
- Software hardwired for the vector processor must be bundled.
- Software for the front-end processor must be priced separately.

Finally, there was a requirement for minimum system availability of 95% on a weekly basis and a mean time to repair to be less than 2 hours.

Hardware Specifications

The computer complex is located in a separate building neighboring all of the Sandia—Albuquerque facilities. To accommodate the added plumbing equipment and power supply required for the CRAY system, fairly extensive changes in the computer building were needed.

Processing, Communication and Terminal Network

Plans for the CRAY-S1000 were to have it service the existing Sandia network shown in Figure 6-2 using one of the CDC 6613 processors to

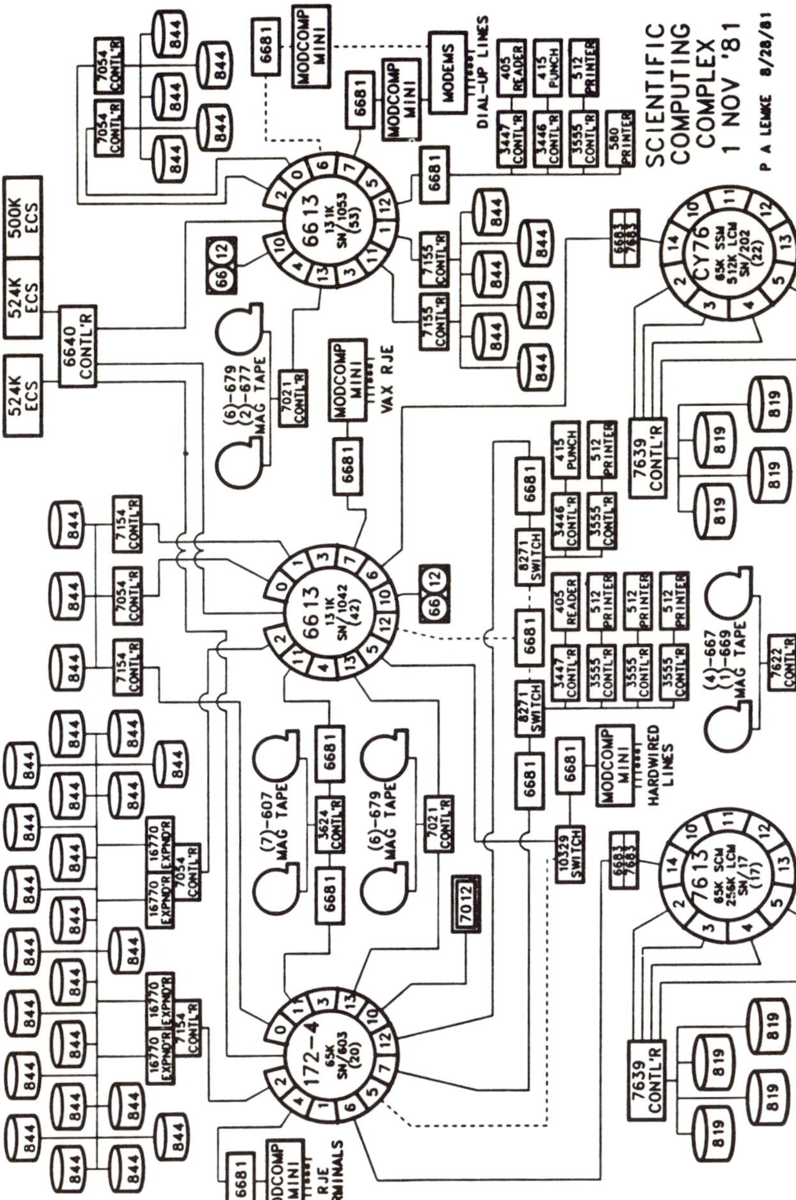

Figure 6-2. Computing network at Sandia Laboratories, Albuquerque, New Mexico (courtesy P. A. Lemke, Sandia National Laboratories).

control access through the job entry terminals. This leaves the CYBER 76 as an alternate high-capacity processor. The expectation was that about 95% of the workload would be handled through remote job entry terminals and about 5% submitted in the computer room. For immediate mass storage needs, eight DD 829 disk units are being purchased to supply an additional 4.8 gigabytes of capacity. However, there is no interactive capability at present in the network. As illustrated by Figure 6.2, the existing system is already a sizable array of equipment. The CRAY processor itself represents a substantial addition.

Unusual Features and Near-Term Plans

The most notable special peripheral equipment is a set of VERSATEC plotters with capabilities in both black and white (printed on microfiche) and color (printed on microfilm). Near-term plans are to install the NSC hyperchannel, as used by LANL, and link the data storage system to the MASSTOR file storage. In the initial use of the CRAY, only batch operation will be performed. The remote access will be implemented through the CDC 172-4 and the CDC 6613 front-end processor.

Software

Operation will depend on the CRAY supplied system software, CFT and COS. COS will be tailored to specific Sandia—Albuquerque needs for security of computer operations and data. No use will be made of CTSS. A major difficulty anticipated is conversion from the internal representation of the CDC 6613 front-end processor, which is CDC 6-bit octal, to the CRAY 8-bit ASCII code.

Level of Satisfaction

Preinstallation support in December 1981 was reported as excellent. This consisted of preparations for hardware installation and assistance with the software already being supplied.

GODDARD LABORATORY FOR ATMOSPHERIC SCIENCE, NATIONAL AERONAUTICS AND SPACE ADMINISTRATION

GLAS, an integral part of NASA, was established in 1977 at the Goddard Space Flight Center in Greenbelt, Maryland, to provide a balanced program of basic and applied research on the earth's atmospheric, hydrospheric and cryospheric systems. (The term cryosphere usually refers to the polar ice caps, glaciers, icebergs and seasonal snow cover.) The main computation facilities in GLAS are managed by the Modeling and Simulation Facility. The GLAS research program emphasizes development of the technology of satellite observation systems, and the atmospheric dynamics models being developed are somewhat specialized.

Description of Systems

To supplement their existing system, based on an Amdahl 470 V/6-1 mainframe, GLAS contracted to have a CDC CYBER 205 Model 200, with a two-pipeline central processor, installed no later than July 24, 1982 with acceptance after initial testing to begin October 24, 1982. Conditions of acquisition were described as "lease payout," but no further details were provided. Although the projected operational life of the CYBER was 6 years, a special contractual requirement guarantees the high-speed processor for 10 years.

Types of Current or Anticipated Use

Three principal elements in the specific mission of the GLAS Modeling and Simulation Facility are:

- development and test of atmospheric and oceanographic models for using and applying comprehensive data sets, emphasizing satellite information;
- broadly based computer-simulated instrument and observing systems tests for assessing expected flight performance; and
- integration of satellite observing systems information into general circulation models (GCM) in research directed toward improved weather, climate and ocean forecasting.

Other groups in GLAS use the computer facilities for photochemical-dynamical models to characterize tropospheric chemical processes, numerical and statistical models based on a merge of remotely sensed and conventional data, and theoretical modeling of climate.

Principal Analytic Applications

There is a great deal of use made of a GCM, which had been developed earlier with the Goddard Institute for Space Studies. As implemented on the Amdahl 470, the GCM is a nine-layer model of the atmosphere horizontally mapped by a grid of 4° latitude and 5° longitude divisions.

Solar and thermal radiation and ground temperature (including the temperature of continental and sea ice) are computed interactively and depend on changing atmospheric temperature and cloud conditions. Current model calculations employ a 10-min time step. It is anticipated that the CYBER 205 will enable the use of somewhat smaller spatial divisions and time steps.

It is hoped that the increased computational capacity will enable GLAS to analyze data from the entire NASA network of ground meteorological stations, five geosynchronous satellites and two polar orbiting satellites for synoptic presentations of atmospheric conditions. It is hoped eventually to combine the global model with upper atmospheric models in treating radiation transfer and atmospheric chemical processes. There are also simulation studies for advanced satellite systems aimed at improving weather and climate forecasting.

In all of the foregoing work, model development would take place in an evolutionary manner so that most of the time the codes would be run for production on a continuing series of new data sets.

Nonanalytic Applications

No administrative loads would be placed on the complex of Amdahl 470 and CYBER 205 systems. However, large amounts of data are being collected by the seven satellites and 4000 ground weather stations worldwide. Before use in analytic models, these data may require some statistical processing. Although there is no thought of real-time analysis at present, the archived data already assembled would be processed through the augmented computer system.

Expected Performance and Criteria of Selection

Provided a set of mandatory minimum standards were met, the selection of a new processor would be judged according to the lowest dollar cost per representative unit calculation over the expected six-year life of the system. The tests for the processors had two important requirements:

- The code of the GCM, with modifications for the vector architecture, must be executed at more than 10 times the speed of the Amdahl 470 V/6-1, as measured by clock time. Six months were allowed for code modifications and trial.
- The same GCM code, without modifications, must be executed in FORTRAN at no less than the speed of the Amdahl 470 V/6-1.

There were 27 other "general purpose" jobs used in the tests. For these, no single job could take more than three times the time required on the

Amdahl and the total 27 no more than two times the requirement of the Amdahl. The new processor and the Amdahl had to be interfaced and be compatible in software. In evaluation of the performance, up to a 20% credit would be added for extra speed. A 20-fold improvement over the Amdahl would gain the whole 20%. There was also an unusual requirement for advance quotation or estimate of the cost to upgrade the processor by a factor of four in the last two years of the system's life. While a single-source prime contractor is responsible for the new system, CDC subcontracted to the Systems Development Corporation for all required equipment not supplied directly by CDC.

Hardware Specifications

The proposed configuration for the GLAS computing facility includes 1 megaword of central memory and 1 gigabyte of disk storage associated with the CYBER 205. While it will be linked to an Amdahl 470 V/6 Model 2 at first, plans include the addition of an Amdahl 470 V/7B. In the final configuration, the V/6 will act as backup support to the V/7B, and the V/7B will function as the front-end processor to the CYBER 205. The CDC Loosely Coupled Network (LCN) is used for system interconnection. Memorex 6250-bpi tape drives are used with the Amdahl systems along with Mass Storage System's M860 subsystem functioning as an automated tape library.

In addition to supporting work at GLAS, the computing facility is also available for modeling and simulation research performed at universities and federal agencies in collaboration with GLAS. The facility includes mass storage provisions of 50 gigabytes, an array of high-speed peripherals, graphics and plotting devices, and a telecommunications network. This network is linked to remote terminals at:

- Harvard University,
- Massachusetts Institute of Technology,
- University of Connecticut,
- University of Maryland,
- New York University,
- University of Wisconsin,
- University of California at Los Angeles,
- Oregon State University, and
- National Meteorological Center of the National Oceanic and Atmospheric Administration (NOAA).

Research with universities accounts for about 40% of the computer's use. At present the computing facility is run on a four-shift, 24-hour daily basis. After installation of the CYBER 205, there should be a need for no more than two shifts to handle the present work load. The remaining two shifts would then be available to outside users on a cost-reimbursable basis.

GEOPHYSICAL FLUID DYNAMICS LABORATORY

GFDL is part of NOAA, which is under the U.S. Department of Commerce. It is located in Princeton, New Jersey, and some Princeton University faculty members and students participate in its research program along with the regular staff members. It was established in 1955 as an adjunct to what was then called the U.S. Weather Service. Its goal is to expand the scientific understanding of the physical processes that govern the behavior of the atmosphere and the oceans as complex fluid systems. These fluids can then be modeled mathematically and their phenomenology studied by computer simulation methods [GFDL 1980].

Description of Systems

Since 1974, GFDL has had unlimited use, for its own research, of the Texas Instruments vector processor, TIX 4 ASC. Texas Instruments built seven of these processors, retaining five of them for its own use. The unit at GFDL has been maintained by Texas Instruments with a staff of about 12 working onsite. However, the company does not want to extend this service beyond September 1982, since they have decided not to enter the supercomputer market. Hence, GFDL decided to replace it before then with a system of at least similar capability.

The federal government signed a "fixed price" contract with CDC for a computer system to be installed at GFDL, to include a CDC CYBER 170/720 as a front-end processor and two CYBER 205 production processors. The front end was delivered and the first CYBER 205 was scheduled for June 1982. It will have 2 megawords of mainframe memory. The second CYBER 205 will follow in April 1984 and will add another 1 megaword of mainframe memory. The system life has been specified as November 1, 1982 to September 30, 1989.

Types of Current or Anticipated Use

GFDL defines the following as its main lines of research:

- predictability of weather, large and small scale;
- particular nature of the earth's atmospheric general circulation within the context of the family of planetary atmospheric types;

- structure, variability, predictability, stability and sensitivity of climate, global and regional;
- structure, variability and dynamics of the ocean over its many space and time scales; and
- interaction of the atmosphere and oceans with each other, and how they influence and are influenced by various trace constituents.

The thrust of this program is very similar to that of the research at GLAS. Absent is the close linkage to a preexistent data network, which, by itself, would tend to govern the spatial and time refinement of theory and analysis. At GFDL these would only be considered according to the requirements for increased understanding of the phenomena being investigated.

Principal Analytic Applications

GFDL also bases much of its work on a GCM developed out of pioneering work in the late 1940s and early 1950s. The nine-layer model of a moist atmosphere, similar to that of GLAS, was largely developed at GFDL [Manabe et al. 1965; Smagorinsky et al. 1965]. Much of the current work at GFDL centers on using the GCM to understand the effects of increased carbon dioxide levels and to simulate atmospheric phenomena on other planets such as Venus, Mars and Jupiter.

Principal Nonanalytic Applications

No nonanalytic applications are planned for the proposed CDC CYBER 205 system.

Expected Performance and Criteria of Selection

For the type of heavily production-oriented programs that have been the main work at GFDL, these processors will double the capacity of the Amdahl or CRAY-1S (averaged over the life of the system). As a combined system, the CDC complex should provide three to five times as much throughput as the TIX 4 ASC. It was pointed out that there will not be a gain in all kinds of capability. The TIX 4 ASC is equipped to operate with one, two or four arithmetic pipes. Each pipe can operate separately, or all can be combined for a large vector. Scalar capability of the CYBER 205 is not expected to be much greater. In vectorizing existing programs, the CDC compiler can only recognize the first level of a FORTRAN nested DO loop, while the TIX 4 ASC can vectorize three levels deep.

The procurement of the new systems, carried out by the U.S. Department of Commerce, attracted three competitors at first: Burroughs, CDC and Cray Research. Burroughs withdrew early; eventually, CDC was awarded the contract. A fixed price was stipulated and the selection criteria were expressed in terms of how much capability, as measured by performance on benchmark problems, could be obtained for that price. Some compiler time was included in the benchmark, but to simulate the actual load, as already experienced at GFDL with a vector processor, the final score was heavily dominated by production capability. Reliability had to be demonstrated or guaranteed to assure that each processor would be available for use 20 hours per day when averaged over a calendar month. Each vendor had to propose the maintenance that would be adequate to meet his guaranteed availability. A production unit, used in the evaluation, represents the work load component typical of the long-running simulations that occupy the system overnight and on weekends. The benchmark tests consisted of four different programs:

- BMARK: stripped-down, atmospheric gridpoint model for a hemisphere of the earth;
- SPTRAL: simple, global, barotropic (one-level) atmospheric model using spherical-harmonic representation for basic variables;
- OCEAN: global, oceanic gridpoint model; and
- PMODEL: complete, global, atmospheric, gridpoint model.

BMARK was to be demonstrated in scalar code on all processors with scalar compiler optimization allowed, but with instructions used to create vector or parallel data structures. All four programs were to be demonstrated on production processors with maximum compiler optimization, including vector or parallel instruction sequences. The calculations carried out were to be at a significance equivalent to at least 10 decimal digits for "real" and "complex" data, and to at least 20 decimal digits for "double precision" data.

OTHER USER ORGANIZATIONS

A number of other user organizations have acquired or are in the process of acquiring vector processors or other advanced computers. These organizations were not accessible for detailed interviews; however, some useful information about their systems and their anticipated applications was obtained.

Boeing Computing Service

The basic configuration for Boeing Computing Service consists of a CRAY-1S processor with 1 megaword of central memory and 12 gigabytes of disk storage. A CDC CYBER 750 serves as a front-end processor. NSC hyperchannel protocol is used. An additional CRAY-1S with 2 megawords of memory was to complete the configuration by December 1981. Most of the applications are proprietary. There is a fair level of use by public service organizations on environmental studies. It is probable that most of the users will rely on the CRAY compiler for any program vectorization.

United Computing Service

The configuration for this user consists of a 1-megaword CRAY-1S processor with 4.8 gigabytes of disk storage. An IBM 3033 serves as a front-end processor. The applications will be very similar to those placed on the Boeing Systems. Again, the public service organizations using it tend to be involved mostly in environmental studies.

Westinghouse Nuclear Energy Center

The system configuration consists of a 1-megaword CRAY-1S system with 9.6 gigabytes of disk storage. A CDC CYBER 720 serves as a front-end processor. Practically all of the applications are in subject areas closely associated with Westinghouse industrial development and production of the pressurized water reactor: nuclear reactor operation, nuclear reactor safety, waste disposal and nuclear fuel cycle.

Cornell University

A HEP system was scheduled for delivery by mid-1982. It will consist of a single process execution module with a 0.25-megaword main memory, 2 megawords of I/O cache memory and 1.6 gigabytes of disk storage. Cornell University has not finalized its hardware requirements and intends to expand the central memory at some point in the future when, it is presumed, memory costs may be lower. The university has a strong program in its graduate physics department for theoretical analysis of fusion plasma dynamics. This will be a major application area. There will also be a variety of programs developed to support the interests of all the graduate scientific departments.

U.S. Air Force North American Defense Command

The proposed system for the U.S. Air Force North American Defense Command is an Amdahl 5860 with 2 megawords of memory. Further details are unavailable. This system will be used to process remotely sensed data from space in conjunction with performing data base operations.

U.S. Air Force Weapons Laboratory

The system for the Air Force Weapons Laboratory is one of the more elaborate. In March 1980 a CRAY-1A was obtained and it has since been upgraded to a CRAY-1S/1000 equipped with 1 megaword of main memory. It is integrated with a CDC 6600 as a front-end processor for batch operations and a Data General Eclipse 200-RDOS for administrative work. There is also an IBM 3031 with 3850 disk drive to operate a mass storage subsystem (35 gigabytes). There are twelve D819 disk drives (3.6 gigabytes) for general storage and eighteen D819 disk drives (4.8 gigabytes) linked to a CTSS for time-sharing. A CYBER 750 operates the communications network. The anticipated life of the CRAY processor is eight years. A major application will be to process remote sensing data from satellites. Already developed application software is run either in the scalar mode, or with use of the CFT for automatic vectorization. There is a problem with a substantial body of PL/I programs since there is at present no CRAY PL/I compiler.

Brookhaven National Laboratory

The proposed Denelcor HEP configuration for this facility will consist of two process execution modules, 0.5 megaword of central memory and 900 megabytes of disk storage. Brookhaven is one of the major national laboratories, managed by a consortium of universities in the Northeast for DOE. The computing system will be applied in six major areas of their basic nuclear energy research programs: nuclear reactor operation, nuclear reactor safety, waste disposal, nuclear fuel cycle, safeguards and fusion. The straightforward features of the Denelcor architecture promise an extra degree of flexibility, which is considered advantageous for a wide variety of computer tasks. This will compensate for the somewhat lower execution speed than either the CRAY-1S or CDC CYBER 205 demonstrated in their benchmark tests.

Knolls Atomic Power Laboratory and Bettis Atomic Power Laboratory

The Knolls and Bettis laboratories are associated, respectively, with General Electric and Westinghouse defense reactor development programs. They have each selected a CDC CYBER 205 for their computing centers. Each is actively concerned with four areas of research and development on fission nuclear reactors: nuclear reactor operation, nuclear reactor safety, waste disposal and nuclear fuel cycle. However, no further information on systems configurations or applications is available, because of the security aspects of their work.

APPENDIX

STANDARD USER SURVEY FORMAT

I. Identification of system
   A. Manufacturer-vendor
   B. Models acquired
      1. Number of units of each type
      2. Specified major levels of capability
      3. Month/year of each acquisition
      4. Anticipated operational lifetime
   C. Conditions of acquisition
      1. Principal finance options and reasons for choice
         a. Direct purchase or rental from vendor
         b. Third-party lease
         c. Lease to ownership (suspendable installments)
      2. Principal terms of agreement
         a. Performance guarantees
         b. Service and maintenance contract
         c. Assistance in initial operation and program conversion

II. Types of anticipated use
   A. Principal analytic applications
      1. Types of computation to be performed and special advantages expected
         a. Frequently used algorithms
         b. Most important mathematical procedures required
         c. Real-time data processing requirements
      2. Source of application programs
         a. In-house
         b. Packaged routines
      3. Level of performance improvement expected and experienced
   B. General administrative applications that may be added as part of service load
   C. Design of any benchmark testing
      1. Specific computational requirements
      2. Evaluation criteria
   D. Special requirements of operating system
   E. Expected job mix

III. Hardware specifications
  A. Location of computer
  B. Major interfaces with other mainframes and input/output (I/O) peripherals
    1. Front-end processor
    2. Central processing unit
    3. Main central memory
    4. Most frequently used peripherals
      a. Disk and tape storage
      b. Printer and card handlers
      c. I/O terminals
      d. Plotting equipment
    5. Data communications
      a. Linkage types
      b. Network design
      c. Interactive capabilities
  C. Mix of local vs remote work stations and terminals
  D. Any unusual peripheral loads linked through other computers
    1. Telecommunications
    2. Special storage systems
    3. Special graphics and printing
    4. Satellite processing systems
  E. Plans for near-term system changes
    1. Modifications
    2. Additional acquisitions

IV. Software configuration
  A. High-level language compilers (numbers and types)
    1. Version
    2. Level of optimization
  B. Assembly language conversion requirements
  C. Operating systems
    1. Batch/interactive capability
    2. Level of multiprogramming (concurrent job execution)
  D. Special applications software packages: name, function, source (in-house, commercial)
  E. Proprietary or classified software level
    1. Manufacturers' packages
    2. Other vendor packages
    3. In-house packages

V. Significant advantages
  A. Response time on specific programs
  B. Ease of system expansion/reconfiguration
  C. Cost vs benefits
  D. Compatibility of prior programs
  E. Compatibility of terminals and other peripherals carried over from prior system
  F. Efficiency of system with respect to required electric power and thermal conditioning

G. Available programming productivity aids
H. Early delivery and/or installation of hardware
I. Early delivery of required software

VI. Significant problem areas
  A. Mismatch of vendor system design to current and near-term projected user requirements
  B. Delay in installation
  C. Delay in required software delivery
  D. Excess system costs
  E. Vendor failure to provide all promised software and other system support
  F. Lack of program/data compatibility
  G. Overly rapid pace of vendor changes in hard- and software
  H. Excessive equipment noise
  I. Excessive power and cooling requirements

VII. Level of satisfaction
  A. Ease of operation
  B. Reliability of mainframe
  C. Maintenance and service
    1. Responsiveness
    2. Effectiveness
  D. Technical support
    1. Troubleshooting
    2. Education programs
    3. Documentation
  E. Manufacturers' software
    1. Operating system
    2. Compilers
    3. Assemblers
    4. Application programs
  F. Ease of programming
  G. Ease of program conversion
  H. Ease of operational conversion

VIII. General commentaries
  A. Did the computer system accomplish what was expected of it? What were its most serious limitations and problems?
  B. What recommendations should be passed on to another prospective user?

REFERENCES

Al-Ayat, R. (1981) "A Model for Analyzing SNM Safeguards Decisions," Energy and Technical Reviews, Lawrence Livermore National Laboratory, Livermore, CA (October), pp. 11-19.

Auerbach (1981a) *Amdahl-580 Series Hardware Report*, 100.1220.872 (Auerbach Publishers, Inc.).

Auerbach (1981b) *CRAY-1S Series Hardware Report*, 100.3004.81 (Auerbach Publishers, Inc.).

Auerbach (1981c) *CYBER 205*, 100.2652.748 (Auerbach Publishers, Inc.).

Auerbach (1981d) *Heterogeneous Element Processor*, 100.3225.200 (Auerbach Publishers, Inc.).

Auerbach (1981e) *Upgrading the Computer* (Auerbach Publishers, Inc.).

Auerbach (1981f) *Basic Architecture for System Control Mechanisms* (Auerbach Publishers, Inc.).

Auerbach (1981g) *Supercomputer and Array Processors* (Auerbach Publishers, Inc.).

Barkai, D. (1981) "Vectorizing the Monte Carlo," Control Data, Ltd., London, UK.

Barnes, D. C., and J. U. Brackbill (1977) "Computation of Megnetohydrodynamic Flow in a Magnetically Confined Plasma," *Nucl. Sci. Eng.* 64:18.

Belzer, R. Z. (1982) Denelcor. Personal communication (January 18).

Berlin, F. B. (1982) Cray Research, Inc. Personal communication (January 18).

Bowring, R. W., J. W. Stewart, P. A. Shober and R. M. Sims (1975) "MEKIN: MIT-EPRI Nuclear Reactor Kinetics Code," EPRI-227, Electric Power Research Institute, Palo Alto, CA.

Branch, M. C., R. J. Kee and J. A. Miller (1981) "A Theoretical Investigation of Mixing Effects in the Selective Reduction of Nature Oxide by Ammonia," SAND81-8836, Sandia National Laboratories, Albuquerque, NM.

Brockway, D. V., and F. Gama-Lobo (1979) "Vectorization Techniques for an Iterative Algorithm," Proceedings of the Conference on Scientific Computer Information Exchange, Livermore, CA, September 12-13.

Bucher, I., and J. W. Moore (1981) "Comparative Performance Evaluation of Two Supercomputers: CDC CYBER 205 and CRI CRAY-1," Computer Measuring Group XII, New Orleans, LA, December 1-4.

Buzbee, B. L. (1981) "Vectorization of Algorithms for Solving Systems of Difference Equations," paper presented at the Conference on Simulation Methods for Nuclear Power Systems, Tucson, AZ, January 26-28.

Buzbee, B. L., G. H. Golub and J. A. Howell (1977) "Vectorization for the Cray-1 of Some Methods for Solving Elliptic Difference Equations," in *High Speed Computer and Algorithm Organizations*, D. J. Kuch, D. H. Lawrie and A. H. Sameh, Eds. (New York: Academic Press, Inc.).

Buzbee, B. L., W. J. Worlton, G. Michael and G. Rodrigque (1980) "DOE Research in Utilization of High-Performance Computers," LA-8609-MS, Los Alamos National Scientific Laboratory, Los Alamos, NM.

Byers, J. A. (1977) "Computer Simulation of Field Reversal in Mirror Machines," *Phys. Rev. Lett.* 39:1476.

Cane, M. A., V. J. Carbone, M. Halem and I. Halberstam (1981) "On the Sensitivity of Numerical Weather Prediction to Remotely Sensed Marine Surface Wind Data: A Simulation Study," *J. Geophys. Res.* 86:8098-8106.

Carlson, G. A. (1978) "Mirror Fusion Reactors," *Energy Technol. Rev.* (September), p. 31.

CDC (1980) "CDC Cyber 200 Model 205 Technical Description," Control Data Corporation.

Datamation (1981) "Look Ahead" (December), p. 13.

Datamation (1982) "Seymour Leaves CRAY" (January 1982), p. 52.

Denelcor (1981a) "Heterogeneous Element Processor: Principles of Operation," Denelcor, Inc.

Denelcor (1981b) "1980 Denelcor Annual Report," Denelcor, Inc.

DOE (1979) "Magnetic Fusion Energy and Computers: The Role of Computing in Magnetic Fusion Energy Research and Development," DOE/ER-0033, Office of Fusion Energy, U.S. Department of Energy, Washington, DC.

Dunn, F. E., and J. M. Kyser (1979) "Impact of Advanced System on LMFBR Accident Analysis Code Development," Proceedings of the Scientific Computer Information Exchange, Livermore, CA, September 12-13.

Dwyer, H. A., R. J. Kee and B. R. Sanders (1980) "Adaptive Grid Method for Problems in Fluid Mechanics and Heat Transfer," *Am. Inst. Aeronaut. Astronaut. J.* 18:1205-1212.

Ewald, R. H., W. J. Worlton and M. McCormick (1981) "Computing Division Two-Year Operational Plan, FY 1981-1982," LA-8725-MS, Los Alamos National Scientific Laboratory, Los Alamos, NM.

GFDL (1980) "Activities—FY 80, Plans—FY 81," Geophysical Fluid Dynamics Laboratory, National Oceanic and Atmospheric Administration, Princeton, NJ.

Halem, M., E. Kalnay-Rivas, W. E. Baker and R. Atlas (1981) "An Assessment of the FGGE Satellite Observing System During DOP-1," Informal Report, Goddard Laboratory for Atmospheric Sciences, Greenbelt, MD.

Hallquist, J. O. (1981) "DYNA3D: Modeling Material Deformation," *Energy Technol. Rev.* (August), pp. 12-21.

Hicks, H. R., and B. Carreras (1979) "Realistic 3D Resistive MHD Calculations on the Cray-1," Proceedings of the Scientific Computer Information Exchange, Livermore, CA, September 12-13.

Hippe, R. (1981) Cray Research, Inc. Personal communication (December 3).

Johnson, P. M. (1978) "An Introduction to Vector Processing," *Computer Design* (February), pp. 89-97.

Kee, R. J., J. A. Miller and T. H. Jefferson (1981) "A Synopsis of Chemkin, A General-Purpose Chemical Kinetics Code," WSS/CI 81-25, paper presented at the Combustion Institute/Western States Spring Meeting, Pullman, WA, April 13-14.

Killeen, J. (1978) "The National MFE Computer Center: Increased Capability in 1978," *Energy Technol. Rev.* (September).

Kneisly, W. A. (1981) Control Data Corporation. Personal communication (October 23).

Kolata, G. B. (1981) "Who Will Build the Next Supercomputer?" *Science* 211:268-269.

Kolodzey, J. S. (1981) "CRAY-1 Computer Technology," *Inst. Electrical Electronics Eng. Trans Components, Hybrids, Mfg. Technol.* CHMT-4(2):181-186.

Levine, R. D. (1982) "Supercomputers," *Scientific Am.* (January), pp. 128-135.

LLL (1978) "National Magnetic Fusion Energy Computer Center," Lawrence Livermore Laboratory, Livermore, CA.

Manabe, S., J. Smagorinsky and R. F. Strickler (1965) "Simulated Climatology of a General Circulation Model with a Hydrologic Cycle," *Monthly Weather Rev.* 43(12):769-798.

Manabe, S., K. Bryan and M. J. Spelman (1979) "A Global Ocean-Atmospheric Climate Model with Seasonal Variation for Future Studies of Climate Sensitivity," *Dynam. Atmos. Oceans* (July 3), pp. 393-426.

Manickam, J. (1979) "CRAY-1 & MHD Stability Studies in Tokamaks," Proceedings of the Scientific Computer Information Exchange, Livermore, CA, September 12-13.

Marx, L. (1979) "Implementation of Vectorizing Techniques on the CDC-Star-100 for Speed Enhancement of GLAS GCM," Proceedings of the Scientific Computer Information Exchange, Livermore, CA, September 12-13.

McCoy, M. G., A. A. Mirin and J. Killeen (1979) "Vectorized Fokker-Planck Package for the CRAY-1," Proceedings of the Scientific Computer Information Exchange, Livermore, CA, September 12-13.

McCraney, R. W. (1971) Cray Research, Inc. Personal communication (October 23).

Miller, J. A., M. C. Branch and R. J. Kee (1981) "A Chemical Kinetic Model for the Selective Reduction of Nitric Oxide by Ammonia," *Combust. Flame* 43:81-98.

Miyakoda, K., J. Smagorinsky, R. F. Strickler and G. D. Hembree (1969) "Experimental Extended Predictions with a Nine-Level Hemispheric Model," *Monthly Weather Rev.* 47(1):1-70.

Moriarity, K. J. M. (1981) "Vectorizing the Monte Carlo," Department of Mathematics, Royal Hollaway College, Egham, Surrey, UK.

Nessett, D., and R. W. Watson (1981) "Improving the Performance of High-Speed Computer Networks," *Energy Technol. Rev.* (February), pp. 16-21.

NRC (1975) "Reactor Safety Study: An Assessment of Accident Risks in U.S.

Commercial Nuclear Power Plants," NUREG 75/014, WASH-1400, U.S. Nuclear Regulatory Commission, Washington, DC.

Orvis, W. H., and J. H. Yee (1981) "Modeling of Solid-State Materials for Solar Cells," *Energy Technol. Rev.* (April), pp. 11-21.

Russell, R. M. (1978) "The CRAY-1 Computer System," *Commun. ACM* (January 1), pp. 63-72.

Sandia (1979) "Justification for Class VI Scientific Computing Capability at Sandia Laboratories, Albuquerque," SAND79-0488, Sandia National Laboratories, Albuquerque, NM.

Simonen, T. C. (1981) "TMX Experimental Results," *Energy Technol. Rev.* (June), pp. 1-9.

Smagorinsky, J., S. Manabe and J. L. Holloway, Jr. (1965) "Numerical Results from a Nine-Level General Circulation Model of the Atmosphere," *Monthly Weather Rev.* 43(12):727-768.

Vigil, J. K., and T. D. Knight (1981) "TRAC Development and Assessment Status," in *Simulation Methods for Nuclear Power Stations*, EPRI WS-81-212 (Palo Alto, CA: Electric Power Research Institute).

Wagner, R. J., Y. H. Ransom and L. J. Ybarrondo (1981) "Potential for Interactive Real Time Nuclear Power Plant Simulation with RELAPS," in *Simulation Methods for Nuclear Power Systems*, EPRI WS-81-212 (Palo Alto, CA: Electric Power Research Institute).

Wheeler, C. L., et al. (1976) "COBRA-IV-I" An Interim Version of COBRA for Thermal-Hydraulic Analysis of Rod Bundle Fuel Elements and Cores," BNWL-1962.

Worlton, J. (1981) "The Philosophy Behind the Machines—Supercomputers," *Computer World* (November 9).

Wulff, W. (1981) "Major Systems Codes, Capabilities and Limitations," in *Simulation Methods for Nuclear Power Systems*, EPRI WS-81-212 (Palo Alto, CA: Electric Power Research Institute).

BIBLIOGRAPHY

AEC (1973) "The Application of Computers to Controlled Thermonuclear Research," WASH-1926, U.S. Atomic Energy Commission, Washington, DC.

Amdahl (1981) "Amdahl-580 Technical Description," Amdahl Corporation.

Auerbach (1980) *Cray Research Inc., Cray-1S Series Overview Report* (Auerbach Publishers, Inc.).

Buzbee, B. L., and A. L. McKnight (1981) "Impact of Vector Processor on Algorithms," Informal Report LA-8123-MS, Los Alamos National Scientific Laboratory, Los Alamos, NM.

Chang, J., M. Ekstrom and F. Fritsch (1976) "Survey of Applied and Computational Mathematics at LLL," Lawrence Livermore Laboratory, Livermore, CA.

Dickenson, A. (1981) "Optimizing Numerical Weather Forecasting Models for the Cray-1 and Cyber 205 Computers," Informal Report, Meteorological Office, Bracknell, Berkshire, UK.

GFDL (1981) "Activities—FY 81, Plans—FY 82," Geophysical Fluid Dynamics Laboratory, National Oceanic and Atmospheric Administration, Princeton, NJ.

Jefferson, T. H., and M. R. Scott (1980) "Megaflop Comparisons of Various Computers," SAND80-2205, Sandia National Laboratories, Albuquerque, NM.

LANL (1981) "Computing at Los Alamos," Los Alamos National Laboratory, Los Alamos, NM.

MIS Week (1981) "Supercomputers Converting Non-science Users" (November 18).

NASA (1980) "Goddard Laboratory for Atmospheric Sciences," Goddard Space Flight Center, National Aeronautics and Space Administration, Greenbelt, MD, p. 30.

Peskin, A. (1981) Brookhaven National Laboratory. Personal communication (October 21).

Rothmund, H. (1981) "3D Implicit Navier-Stokes Code on the Control Data Cyber 205 Computer," Informal Report, Control Data Corporation.

Sandia (1977) "Sandia Laboratories, Livermore Computer Needs," SAND77-0015, Sandia National Laboratories, Albuquerque, NM.

Shuttleworth, B. O. (1977) "A Documentary of MFENET, a National Computer Network," UCRL-53317, Lawrence Livermore Laboratory, Livermore, CA.

SECTION 2

BIOCHIP TECHNOLOGY

CHAPTER 7

INTRODUCTION AND OVERVIEW

Futurists predict that two new and far-reaching technologies, very large-scale integrated (VLSI) circuits and biotechnology, will dominate industrial innovation and development over the remainder of this century. For the past 20 years, the semiconductor industry has led an industrial revolution of sorts by producing electronic devices that have had a profound effect on the quality of life. The integrated circuit (semiconductor chip) has made possible huge reductions in the size, cost and power requirements of electronic equipment, and is now incorporated in common household appliances and the most sophisticated computers and telecommunications systems. Biotechnology, particularly recombinant DNA technology (splicing genes from different organisms), is equally promising in terms of potential impact; however, the technology is less than 10 years old and the first commercial products (pharmaceuticals) are not yet on the market. The potential exists, however, to assemble the genetic code for producing new substances (e.g., drugs, food products and chemicals) that are not available in nature and for improving the efficiency of existing industrial processes, ranging from mining to pollution control.

It has recently occurred to researchers in both biotechnology and microelectronics that the two technologies may be combined to allow the use of biological materials and processes in the design and fabrication of microelectronic devices. Bioelectronics, therefore, represents a convergence of (1) the need in microelectronics for ever-increasing density of circuit elements, and (2) the inherent capacity of biological systems to transport electrons on a molecular scale. The semiconductor industry, under current photolithographic methods of fabrication, will reach the fundamental limits after only two or three more doublings in circuit density. Moreover, as these maximum densities are approached, the proportion of manufacturing defects will increase, necessitating costly quality assurance procedures. Among the proposed new approaches to device fabrication, the use of biological materials and technology is the most revolutionary and far-reaching in its departure from conventional microelectronics.

Section 2 of this book surveys bioelectronics. The first objective is to describe briefly the current state-of-the-art of bioelectronics. Since the field is at an early stage, emphasis is placed on including the entire range of concepts encompassed by this new area. The second objective is to project future trends in bioelectronics in terms of the anticipated technical advances and the response of the industry to future research and development (R&D) needs.

An overview is provided of the current state-of-the-art, major technical hurdles and likely development schedules in bioelectronics. Three aspects of bioelectronics are included:

1. biological processes and materials in device fabrication: recent developments in the use of protein and other biological materials;
2. molecular circuitry: conceptual designs for three-dimensional devices that mimic biochemical electron transport; and
3. biosensors: field-effect transistors (FET) that sense and respond to the electric potential created by the products of biochemical reactions.

The future outlook for bioelectronics is discussed in Chapter 9 in terms of the innovation process and R&D strategies for microelectronics in general.

OVERVIEW OF THE TECHNOLOGY

What follows are brief descriptions of recent developments in three areas of bioelectronics. The limited scope of this survey and the newness of much of the research preclude in-depth consideration of each technology. The information presented in this section is derived from the technical literature, patents and discussions with researchers. Two meetings on the subject of biotechnology and microelectronics are noteworthy:

- "Genetic Engineering Comes to Microelectronics," a seminar presentation by J. H. McAlear, EMV Associates, Inc., sponsored by the Institution of Electrical and Electronics Engineers (IEEE) Washington Section, January 11, 1982; and
- "Interagency Conference on Biomolecular Electronics," sponsored by the National Science Foundation (NSF), May 26, 1982 [McAlear 1982b].

A one-day seminar was conducted on April 15, 1982, at The MITRE Corporation, with representatives from EMV Associates, Inc., to gain first-hand insight into current R&D [McAlear 1982a].

Biological Processes and Materials in Device Fabrication

The evolution of microelectronics technology over the past 30 years has been characterized by two major advances—the transistor (ca. 1950), and the integrated circuit (ca. 1960). Each development was followed by refinements leading to smaller components performing increasingly complex functions at greater speeds. This effort at miniaturizing electronic components was initially a response to the needs of military and space agencies in the 1950s for complex electronic systems with minimal size, power and weight requirements. In addition, the success of the transistor as a substitute for the vacuum tube spawned research into alternative materials that could allow various electronic functions to be performed within a solid. This research coincided with the advent of the stored-program digital computer as another large potential market for miniaturized electronic devices. Ultimately, the integrated circuit was developed to allow the interconnection of transistors and other circuit elements on miniature wafers.

Since the early 1960s, progress in microelectronics technology has been astonishing. The area on a silicon chip required for a given electronic logic has been halved every 18 months, and the cost per unit of memory has been declining in a similar fashion. By the 1970s, the scale of integration had increased to the point where a chip 0.25 in. square could hold more electronic elements than the most complex electronic device that could be built in 1950. From the viewpoint of those involved in the design and fabrication of such devices, the appreciation of their complexity is probably related more to the technical difficulties in producing error-free devices than in the functions those devices perform. Modern integrated circuits are designed by large teams using computer-aided design facilities, because the sheer quantity of information exceeds the limits of intuitive engineering. Despite increases in packing density, the requirement for completely error-free layout remains; in this sense, the future potential of microelectronics depends on the development of new design and fabrication technology that can handle such complexity.

As new applications for microelectronics have been introduced, and the demand for devices has increased, the industry has been able to respond with the necessary improvements in fabrication technology. However, fundamental limits imposed by the laws of physics will soon be reached, and further doublings in density are likely to result in an increased probability of defects in manufacture. Modifications in fabrication techniques necessary to assure defect-free devices may reverse the trend of the past 20 years and result in increasing cost per function or bit of memory.

The inevitability of soon reaching the limits, both theoretical and economic, of current photolithographic fabrication techniques has led the microelectronics industry to explore new approaches, including electron beam etching, monolayer deposition of gallium arsenide and construction of Josephson junction switches. It is in this context that bioelectronics, the use of biological techniques and materials in the construction of electronic devices, has received much recent popular attention [Bussert 1982; McAuliffe 1981; Pollack 1982] as the most revolutionary departure from conventional microelectronics. To some extent, this popular attention is due to the speculative future applications of bioelectronics (e.g., electronic brain implants to restore sight to the blind and self-assembling biological computers). As with many developmental technologies, however, early progress in the form of prototype devices will be necessary to assure continued interest and financial support for the research necessary to achieve the above goals.

The importance of actually constructing a prototype to demonstrate new concepts in microelectronics is apparent in the development of the transistor—a device that revolutionized electronics. Although the first transistor developed at Bell Laboratories was a very crude device and inferior to the vacuum tubes then in use, it served two important purposes:

- demonstrating the "transistor effect" (use of a semiconductor crystal to both amplify and rectify a current) in an actual working device; and
- indicating the future potential of a device that consumes very little energy, thus providing a solution to the heat generation problems of vacuum tubes.

Subsequent refinements led to the substitution of the transistor for the vacuum tube and the start of the semiconductor era in electronics.

Today, researchers in microelectronics are faced with a similar challenge—to develop prototypes that demonstrate the feasibility and inherent advantages of new device concepts. In this section, efforts at defining and demonstrating the feasibility of using biological processes and materials in constructing an electronic device, a "biochip," will be summarized and future prospects evaluated.

State-of-the-Art Summary

The ultimate objective of bioelectronics research is to mimic molecular-level electron transfer in nature. Before this objective can be reached, however, the basic materials and techniques for constructing a very small device (VSD) must be investigated. Recent R&D, therefore, has centered on two fundamentals:

- use of technique developed in ultracytochemistry to deposit very thin metal lines in a protein matrix; and
- orientation of a protein monolayer or other substrate to lead to a subassembly of macromolecules that will form an electronic circuit.

The work described below has not resulted in an operational electronic device (a biochip). It does, however, provide a conceptual approach to constructing biochips and demonstrates some of the possible fabrication techniques and materials.

As indicated above, the basic approach to biochip fabrication, at its current stage of development, is based on metal-binding reactions developed in ultracytochemistry—that is, heavy metal staining of microstructures within cells so that they can be detected with an electron microscope. More specifically, it has been demonstrated that silver lines on the order of 4 μm in width can be deposited by electron beam writing on a protein-resist composite, followed by binding of silver to exposed free amino groups in the protein. The three basic steps involved are [McAlear and Wehrung 1981]:

1. Production of protein-resist composite: the synthetic protein polylysine is adsorbed onto a glass slide, which is then coated with the resist compound, polymethyl methacrylate (PMMA).
2. Electron beam writing: line patterns are traced on the resist by a direct-writing electron beam [e.g., a computer-controlled scanning electron microscope (SEM)].
3. Silver deposition: the exposed areas of resist are dissolved in alcohol to uncover lanes of polylysine, and a silver nitrate stain is applied resulting in binding of metallic silver to the exposed polylysine.

Figure 7-1 is a scanning electron micrograph demonstrating that continuous silver lines, approximately 4 μm wide, are deposited on the substrate in the parallel line pattern traced by the electron beam.

The work to date by EMV Associates has emphasized developing the techniques of fabrication rather than constructing an actual working device. The method described above, however, demonstrates the possibility of depositing a conductor using reactions developed in the field of ultracytochemistry, in a pattern determined by electron beam writing on a protein-resist complex. Variations on this approach to device fabrication are discussed in two patents [McAlear and Wehrung 1978a,b]. Materials other than metals can be deposited, and more complex micropatterns can be drawn; examples include:

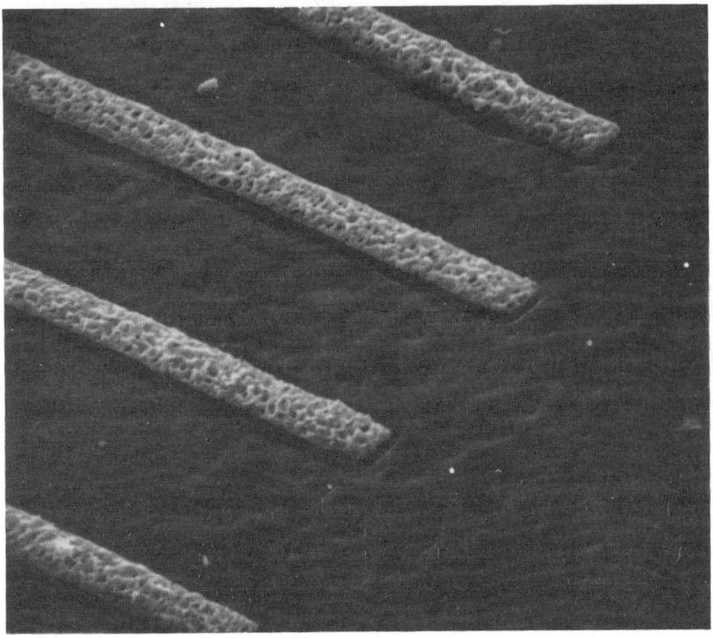

Figure 7-1. Scanning electron micrograph of silver lines 4 μm wide deposited on protein substrate [McAlear and Wehrung 1981].

- deposition of metal oxide films or alloy films as resistive circuit elements;
- introduction of dopants through conventional diffusion furnace techniques;
- application of dielectric materials; and
- attachment of enzymes and other protein structures to the free amino groups of the protein monolayer.

What follows is a step-by-step summary of the latter approach, in this case, attachment of an enzyme-labeled macromolecule to an electric field-oriented protein monolayer [McAlear and Wehrung 1978a]:

1. A solution of the protein cytochrome C is prepared as a monolayer by flowing it onto a water surface in a Langmuir trough and compressing under a glass bar.
2. The molecules of cytochrome C are induced into a grid-like array by subjecting the monolayer to a high-voltage, low-amperage, direct-current electric field.
3. A solution of anticytochrome C phosphatase-labeled antibody is introduced so that one molecule of the antibody is attached to each antigenic site presented by the cytochrome C monolayer.
4. The monolayer is lifted by securing it to a silicon wafer, the hydrophobic side of each protein molecule adhering to the wafer, and the monolayer is then covered with a PMMA mask film.

The product after step 4 is a microsubstrate comprised of (1) a supporting layer of protein (cytochrome C) in which the macromolecules have been organized into a known stereospecific spatial pattern; and (2) a corresponding pattern-building protein, the phosphatase-labeled antibody. A number of steps (e.g., positive or negative masking) can be undertaken at this point to take advantage of the above micropattern. These steps might be:

- A negative mask area can be defined by subjecting this area to irradiation with a focused electron beam at a heavy dosage level—this irradiation deactivates the enzyme and partially depolymerizes the PMMA.
- Lead can then be deposited at the remaining active sites by reacting the phosphatase with creatinine phosphate to yield phosphate ions, reacting the liberated phosphate with lead nitrate, and thermally reducing the resulting lead phosphate to yield metallic lead.

In an effort to further demonstrate the potential advantages of the biochip concept and to arrive at an early prototype, other existing ordered biological systems are being investigated. Striated muscle, for example, represents a three-dimensional lattice arrangement of filaments that has been well studied from a structural and functional viewpoint and, therefore, is currently under consideration as a new material for biochip development [McAlear 1982a]. In the proposed device, an ultrathin section of a sarcomere (Figure 7-2), the structural and functional unit responsible for muscle contraction, is attached to the same silicon-protein substrate developed in the work described above, etched, and stained with a metal. It is anticipated that the arrays of thick and thin filaments, once stained with the metal, would represent a structure analogous to a superlattice, and an electron tunneling phenomenon could be observed once a current is introduced.

As mentioned at the outset of this section, the primary objective at this stage of biochip development is to construct prototypes that demonstrate new materials and fabrication technologies and to establish the feasibility of electronic devices based on biotechnology. As with the first transistor, these prototype biochips are not designed to outperform current integrated circuit chips, but to demonstrate the potential for a new era in microelectronics. The state-of-the-art in biochip research is summarized in Table 7-1.

Future Outlook

The direction of future research and development in biochips will be determined by a combination of (1) technical and scientific advances, and

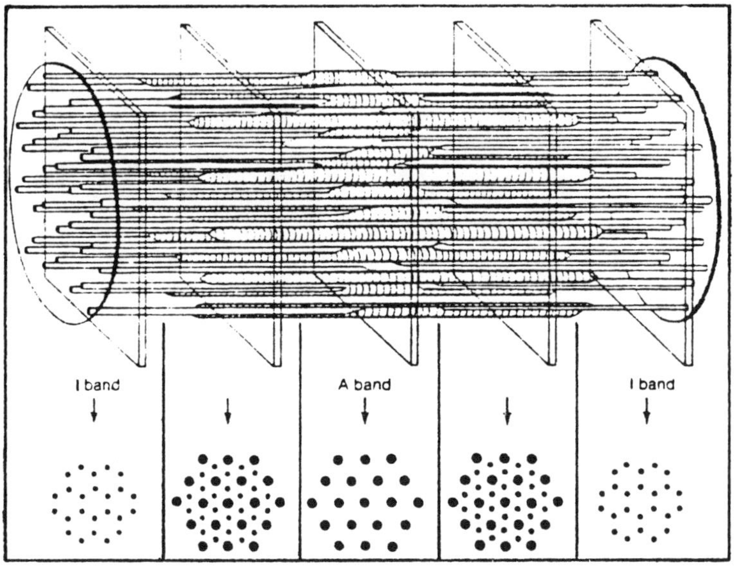

Figure 7-2. Sarcomere [Huxley 1958].

(2) the demand for electronic circuitry of diminishing size and increasing complexity, reliability and speed. As mentioned earlier, this demand has existed since the advent of the integrated circuit in the 1960s, and the microclcctronics industry has responded with a doubling in circuit density every 18 months while the cost per unit of memory has decreased along a roughly parallel curve. As fundamental limits of current lithographic fabrication methods are reached, the demand for increased circuit density and performance will be met with increasing unit cost, due to the costly procedures necessary to assure defect-free devices. The future outlook for biochip technology, therefore, must be viewed in terms of the scientific and economic factors affecting microelectronics R&D in general.

Since the computing industry is likely to remain the major driving force for miniaturization in electronics, it is useful to examine the future needs of that industry beyond increased packing density. With the technology to mass-produce chips containing tens of thousands of circuit elements, it now costs far more to assemble these chips onto printed circuit boards, tests and then combine these boards into a computer than does producing chips. This cost differential is a function of the two-dimensional nature of state-of-the-art device design and computer architecture. Another concern is the operating speed of the computer: with two-dimensional structures, speed is limited by the length of wiring needed to connect

Table 7-1. State-of-the-Art Summary: Biochips

Technique/Concept	Current Status	Remarks
Protein monolayer	Use of Langmuir trough with polylysine has been demonstrated	Other proteins have been proposed (e.g., cytochrome)
Orientation of monolayer	Concept developed and patented	Basic substrate for future molecular devices
Protein-resist composite	Demonstrated using PMMA	Other resist materials could be used that are deposited by irradiation
Direct electron beam writing and metal deposition	Demonstrated using conventional techniques of electron beam lithography; deposition or enzyme-mediated	General problems with electron beam lithography apply (slow and difficult to control with adequate precision)
Use of muscle filament as a superlattice analog	Concept proposed, work not yet initiated	Represents another prototype to demonstrate concepts; not envisioned as a commercial device
Interconnections with external contacts [e.g., leads to power source, input/output (I/O) device]	Not yet demonstrated	A practical solution to the problem on interfacing with elements at the submicrometer scale has not yet been offered (theoretical work is discussed in the section on biosensors)
Use of computer modeling to select proteins with specific three-dimensional structures to organize molecular logic and switching functions	Concept proposed; extensive use of computer modeling not yet initiated	Represents a necessary step to increase the range of molecules that may be used in construction of biochips
Use of recombinant DNA technology to produce computer-modeled sequences	Feasible with current state of genetic technology	Recombinant DNA methods make it feasible to fabricate three-dimensional molecular logic with structures that would otherwise be unavailable from conventional synthetic routes
New system concepts and/or applications	Theoretical studies only	Radically different approaches to device design and system architecture may be required to account for cooperative effects and noise

individual chips. Finally, as more resistive circuit elements are packed into the components, heat dissipation becomes a limiting factor in computer design and performance.

To respond to the above needs, future R&D in microelectronics will have to address more than simply further increasing the amount of logic that can be written on a chip using lithography. The current and 1990 projected practical limits of lithography are presented in Table 7-2 in terms of two important criteria [Wohtjen 1981]:

- resolution: the minimum feature size, and
- registration: the precision with which features can be aligned as layers are fabricated on top of each other.

As resolution in the nanometer range is approached with electron and ion beam lithography, problems will arise including registration errors and the time and computer memory storage required to operate the lithography system. As described by Wohtjen [1981], an ion beam system with a resolution of 1 nm would require approximately 2.0×10^{11} bytes of memory and a writing time of nearly 7 hours to describe a pattern that covers 10% of a 5-mm^2 chip (Table 7-3). This type of fabrication, therefore, is too slow and error-ridden to be commercially feasible, although its use in R&D will continue to be important.

Solutions to the problems of cost of fabrication, speed and heat dissipation are being sought in R&D on new materials, fabrication methods and three-dimensional device design. The object of biochip research is to capitalize on the inherent advantages of biological systems such as:

Table 7-2. Current and Projected Future Performance of Existing Lithographic Techniques[a]

	Resolution (μm)		Registration (μm)	
Lithography System	**Present**	**1990**	**Present**	**1990**
Optical	1.5	0.75	0.5	0.1
Ultraviolet	0.5	0.25	0.25	0.1
X-Ray	0.1[b]	0.01[b]	0.1	0.005[c]
Scanned Electron Beam	0.1	0.0005	0.1	0.005[c]
Scanned Ion Beam	0.1	0.001	0.1	0.005[c]

[a] Adapted from Wohltjen [1981]. Values represent limits on day-to-day commercial operation and do not represent absolute limits of the technology.
[b] Limited by mask resolution.
[c] Limited by substrate stability.

Table 7-3. Current and Projected Future Limitations of Ion Beam Lithography[a]

	Present	1990
Resolution (μm)	0.1	0.001
Registration Error (μm)	0.1	0.005
Writing Time, 5- × 5-mm chip, 10%	25 sec	6.9 hr
Pattern Data[b] Storage Capacity (bytes)	2.0×10^7	2.0×10^{11}

[a]Adapted from Wohltjen [1981].
[b]Assuming 8 bytes/shape and average shape = 100 beam steps.

- small dimensions,
- low resistance and power requirement,
- nondissipative conduction, and
- ability to self-assemble in three dimensions.

The state-of-the-art research summarized above represents a first step toward fabrication of three-dimensional molecular-scale devices. The oriented protein monolayers currently developed may form the basic substrate for future devices. In addition, a sequence of events, such as those listed in Table 7-4, is likely to occur through the year 2000. Taking the three periods of time depicted in Table 7-4 (1985–1987, 1988–1992 and 1993–2000), three phases of biochip development can be identified as follows:

- Phase I: demonstration of near-term results through development of prototypes based on known, organized biological structures (e.g., muscle filament);
- Phase II: development of the knowledge base necessary for the ultimate technology of biochip construction (i.e., computer modeling of protein structure, theoretical designs of molecular logic elements and refined fabrication technology); and
- Phase III: construction of a prototype device based on molecular subassembly that incorporates the techniques developed in earlier phases (e.g., oriented protein substrated and computer modeling) with recombinant DNA technology.

The time frame depicted in Table 7-4 assumes adequate interest and funding of R&D, and successful resolution of key technical barriers (e.g., successful demonstration of a molecular switching mechanism).

A list of some of the persons and organizations currently involved in biochip R&D in the United States is provided in Table 7-5. At the present time, limited resources are being applied to exploratory investigations. According to one projection, an estimated $60 million is required over the next 2–5 years based on the scenario outlined in Table 7-4, and the number of groups involved is likely to expand from currently less than 20 to nearly 100 over that time period [McAlear 1982a].

These and much greater future increases in the scope of R&D will

Table 7-4. Major Developments in Biochip Fabrication Technology Projected to the Year 2000

	Milestone	Importance
1985–1987	Refined technology for production of oriented substrate	Demonstrate commercial feasibility of experimental procedures
	Development of a library of natural proteins and monoclonal antibodies	This information would provide a sufficient variety of molecular structures to fabricate three-dimensional arrays on the oriented monolayer; this information would also be used in computer modeling of chemical structure
	Improved resolution in electron and ion beam lithography	Resolution at the nanometer level will allow further development of prototype devices; the amount of information storage required in the computer control for the lithography systems may exceed practical limits
	Use of myocin filament in device fabrication	Demonstrate another example of an electronic device using an organized biological system
1988–1992	Computer modeling of three-dimensional structures	Allow fabrication of three-dimensional arrays with specified geometries and bonding characteristics to organize molecular switching mechanisms
	Design and first prototype of a molecular switching mechanism	Combination of theoretical work on molecular electronics and practical work on development of oriented protein substrate resulting in a prototype molecular logic device
	Practical improvements in stability and realiability of first prototypes	Improve performance of first prototypes toward objective of a commercially feasible technology
1993–2000	Refinement of molecular switching and logic mechanism	Improvement of earlier designs to resolve problems of noise, substrate stability, etc.
	Use of genetic engineering to produce some of the molecular components	Based on an ability to predict structure from animo acid sequence, recombinant DNA technology could be used to program microorganisms to produce the required structure metabolically
	Development of interconnections to external contacts for I/O	Essential for practical application of molecular devices
	New system concepts for applications of biochips	In order to use three-dimensional molecular logic, new approaches to the basic design of systems will have to be developed, e.g., parallel processing, cooperative effects and faster data I/O

Table 7-5. Partial List of Persons and/or Organizations in the United States Involved in Biochip Development

Organization	Principal Contact	Involvement
EMV Associates, Inc., Rockville, MD	J. H. McAlear; J. M. Wehrung	Materials and fabrication technology; special applications (e.g., implants for eyesight restoration)
University of North Carolina, Chapel Hill, NC	J. Hanker	Metals deposition by biochemical reaction (in collaboration with EMV Associates)
Genex Corp., Rockville, MD	K. Ulmer	Applications of genetic engineering to microelectronics
Naval Research Laboratory, Washington, DC	F. Carter	Development of molecular switching mechanisms
National Science Foundation, Washington, DC	H. Grayber	Funding research in the applications of biotechnology to microelectronics
Office of Naval Research, Arlington, VA	P. Daily	Research programs in biomolecular engineering
IBM, Yorktown Heights, NY	A. Aviram	Molecular information storage
University of Mississippi, University, MS	R. Metzger	Development of molecular switching mechanism

depend on the second of the two factors mentioned above: successful resolution of major technical barriers. Major barriers are critical links in technology development that cannot be resolved without a significant advancement beyond current state-of-the-art. The major barriers to a commercially feasible molecular-scale device include:

- design of a workable molecular switching mechanism;
- fabrication of the above in a stable medium;
- control of and access to the molecular circuitry (e.g., crosstalk phenomena and connections to the outside world); and
- development of new system architectures to use biochips.

The solutions to some of these problems will have to be developed using the limited funds of exploratory research programs such as those at EMV Associates or the Naval Research Laboratory before large-scale testing and development efforts can be initiated.

Molecular Circuitry

The ultimate objective of biochip research is to mimic molecular-level information processors in nature. The research described above focuses on the materials and methods problems associated with constructing a device (a biochip) that can achieve this objective of molecular-scale operation. In a simple analogy, this work might be viewed as development of the "mortar and bricks" to be used in constructing a building for which only general specifications are available. Based on this analogy, the building can be constructed only after design specifications (the "blueprints") are developed in detail. In biochip research, there is an alternative approach to the "materials and methods of construction" school. This approach involves theoretical examination of molecular structures that could process electrical current and eventually be incorporated into a molecular-scale electronic device (i.e., the design of molecular circuitry).

The two approaches, therefore, are directed at the same objective: the materials and methods approach will lead to subassembled macromolecules providing the basic supporting structure of a molecular device; the theoretical approach will provide the molecular logic to be incorporated in that structure. The following section briefly describes a sample of the research related to molecular circuits. It is beyond the scope of this survey to describe in detail these theoretical studies.

State-of-the-Art Summary

Research on molecular circuits and switches has been, without exception, speculative, i.e., no artificial molecular switches have been announced in the literature. However, a number of theoretical studies are directed at the development of such devices. A representative sampling of studies that examine biological systems in particular is presented in Table 7-6. Due to the early stage of much of this research, and the relatively recent expansion of interest, the best sources of state-of-the-art information are recent conferences. The Workshop on Molecular Electronic Devices held at the Naval Research Laboratory in Washington, DC on March 23–24, 1981 is the most recent source of published information [Carter 1981a,b], and provides additional detail on much of the work represented in Table 7-6.

In addition to biological systems, such as those included in Table 7-6, a number of researchers are exploring nonbiological models for molecular switching. Much of this work developed out of work over the past decade on electroactive polymers and a proposed model for an organic chemical rectifier patented by Aviram and Seiden [1974]. Examples of recent studies include the following:

- evaluation of the suitability of hemiquinones as molecular information storage systems [Aviram et al. 1981];
- electron tunnel and soliton propagation phenomena, which offer the potential, respectively, of speed-of-light signal transport and high component density (e.g., 10^{18} elements/cm^3) [Carter 1981c].

At this stage, studies such as the above do not attempt to resolve issues such as access to molecular switches, the support structure or environment of the switch, performance testing, or even the synthesis of the desired structures. More detailed information on the state-of-the-art of molecular electronic devices can be found in Carter [1981a,b] and McAlear and Wehrung [1982].

Future Outlook

Research in molecular electronic devices is likely to accelerate over the next 5–10 years as theoretical switching mechanisms are successfully demonstrated in the laboratory. The state-of-the-art is likely to benefit, as well, from new research thrusts in the related fields of superconducting organic crystals and conducting polymers.

The problems of noise, cooperative effects, heat dissipation, stability, control and necessary system architecture all affect the development of molecular switches. The time frames depicted in Table 7-4 are also applicable:

- a demonstrated switching mechanism within 5–10 years, and
- within 20 years, refinements to the above and a greater availability of molecular

Table 7-6. Examples of Research on Biomolecular Switching

Biological System	Example/Remarks	Reference
Photosynthetic Apparatus	Part of the electron transfer in photosynthesis is facilitated by quinones; transferring the operating principles of this system to an artificial device would require control of unwanted electron transfer and proton uptake	Shipman 1981
Microtubules	Microtubules are cylindrical protein polymers found in all living cells that may have an important role in cellular communication and information processing; preliminary research is underway to see if they could be a useful model for artificial molecular devices	Hameroff and Watt 1981
Porphyrins	Porphyrins are components of important biomolecules, such as hemoglobin and chlorophyll, that incorporate metal ions in their structure; with the proper molecular conformation, the molecules could act as a molecular circuit with switching in the form of paramagnetic resonance induced by visible light	Barrett 1981; Ulmer 1981
Visual Pigments	The pigment system leading to vision is analogous to a switching device, in that it absorbs photons and forms photoproducts in a reversible reaction in which the two states can be distinguished by their spectral and potential differences	Honig 1981

structures through the combination of computer modeling and recombinant DNA technology.

As progress is made toward achieving molecular logic, increasing emphasis will have to be placed on the problem of designing circuits with such fundamental complexity. This issue is discussed further in Chapter 8.

Biosensors

One of the most important applications of biotechnology to microelectronics is the development of sensing devices. These devices, a type of FET, are based on conventional silicon gate technology, but rather than responding to externally applied fields, they sense and respond to the electric potential created by selected ions (ion-selective FET) or by the polar structure of neutral molecules (chem FET). The contribution of biotechnology to this area is in the use of bacteria, enzymes or antibodies in the sensing medium of the FET.

FET are constructed by embedding a silicon chip or other semiconductor material in a nonreactive epoxy resin and surrounding it with a sensing fluid enclosed in a membrane. The fluid carries current to the chip surface (a gate electrode) based on its electrical characteristics which, in turn, are related to the nature of the substance(s) being sensed. The main advantages of such sensing devices include:

- small size,
- sensitivity,
- selectivity, and
- ruggedness.

The state-of-the-art in the use of biological processes and materials in FET technology is summarized below along with future prospects for R&D and commercial application.

State-of-the-Art Summary

There has been increasing interest over the past decade in merging biotechnology with FET technology to arrive at a new generation of sensing devices. R&D in this area is driven, to a large extent, by the specific requirements of individual sensing applications. For example, the need to detect nerve gases used in chemical warfare led to the development of chem FET based on the enzyme system that the nerve poison affects. The state-of-the-art, therefore, is best defined in terms of the types of applications for which the technology is being developed. These applications include:

- biomedical, e.g., heart monitoring and blood analysis;
- industrial, e.g., corrosion in pipes and tanks, and fermenter monitoring;
- environmental, e.g., water and air quality monitoring; and
- defense, e.g., chemical and biological defense systems.

Examples from each of the above application areas are discussed below and summarized in Table 7-7.

Biomedical Applications. Effective treatment of diabetes depends on finely regulated administration of insulin to maintain the proper blood levels of insulin and glucose. The sensitivity and continuous monitoring features of chem FET are being exploited in the development of automated devices to control glucose blood levels. One version [Albisser and Leibel 1978] involves a closed-loop system that samples blood, analyzes for glucose and regulates the delivery of insulin to the patient. Glucose concentration is measured using a glucose oxidase enzyme reaction. Although the system described by Albisser and Leibel [1978] is limited to bedside use, others have developed miniaturized, implantable devices to perform the same function.

The human body contains a variety of proteins, including structural and contractile materials, antibodies, transport molecules, such as hemoglobin, and a number of hormones. The concentrations of these substances are important diagnostic indicators; however, conventional analysis methods, such as immunoassay, are difficult and expensive. Schenck [1980] describes a chem FET device that senses particular proteins in solution. Instead of the metallic gate electrode of conventional FET, however, a monomolecular layer of an antibody protein specific to an antigenic protein to be detected is adsorbed onto the insulating layer. The charge at this gate region is altered by the reaction between the antigen and antibody, thus altering the drain to source current in the transistor. The time rate of change of this current is a measure of the concentration in solution of the antigenic protein being detected. The inventors have also proposed a multiple detection device in which a number of gate regions are constructed with particular antibodies. By measuring current through each of these drain contacts, two or more antigenic proteins can be measured simultaneously. This type of device may have a number of applications, including:

- detection of antibodies and antigens associated with infectious disease (to measure

Table 7-7. State-of-the-Art Summary: Biosensors

Application Area	Technique/Concept	Remarks
Biomedical	Continuous monitoring of blood electrolytes	Current laboratory analysis takes too long (at least 15 min) to be useful in emergency situations; current proposals are for the use of conventional ion-selective FET, rather than biological chem FET
	Measurement of serum proteins	Chem FET based on antibody-antigen reactions; potentially useful tool for diagnosis
	Automated control of glucose blood levels	Chem FET for detecting glucose can be integrated with a feedback system for delivering insulin to diabetics
Industrial	Reaction monitoring	FET can be devised to detect a number of reaction products and by-products, including NH_3, NH_4, H_2, penicillin and glucose
	Corrosion detection	A FET with embedded sulfate-reducing bacteria has been proposed as an early warning device for corrosion in pipes and oil tanks
Environmental	Ambient water and air monitoring	FET could be devised for detection of trace amounts of highly toxic substances in air and water; devices developed for chemical warfare purposes are currently sensitive to 1 ppb of organophosphate insecticides
	Industrial hygiene monitoring	Biosensors could be used to detect exposure to hazardous substances in the workplace (the concept of a biosensor may be traced back to the use of canaries by miners to detect toxic gases)
	Indoor air pollution	The hazards posed by indoor air pollution are often a result of chronic exposure to trace amounts of pollutants. It is conceivable that low-cost FET could be developed as alarm devices for the presence of these pollutants
Defense	Chemical and biological warfare	Defense against chemical and biological warfare agents requires effective means of rapidly detecting harmful levels of these substances under field conditions. R&D has focused on FET based on the mechanism of action of the agent (e.g., the cholinesterase enzyme system for organophosphorus compounds)

antibody concentration, the gate region of the device would be coated with antigen rather than antibody);
- measurement of hormone concentrations to detect endocrine system disorders; and
- mass screening of patients to detect patterns in serum protein levels.

Giaever [1974] developed a device that detects, at low concentrations, biological particles such as viruses, bacteria and other cells in solution. As with the previous example, a monomolecular layer of antibodies specific to the particle to be detected is deposited on a substrate. After being immersed in physiologic fluid containing the particles, the structure is coated with a layer of nonetchable metal that does not, however, completely coat the biological particles bonded to the antibodies. After exposure to an etchant bath, which dissolves the particles and the underlying antibodies, the structure is examined visually and points at which particles had been bonded are observed as voids in the otherwise nonetchable metal layer. Although this device is not a FET (no current detection is involved) it is possible that it could be modified to operate in similar fashion to the device developed by Schenck [1980]. In this case, particles such as viruses would be detected, rather than individual protein molecules.

Industrial Applications. Control of fermentation processes depends on frequent monitoring of the amount of product in the reactor. In the production of penicillin, enzyme electrodes have been developed in which the enzyme penicillinase is immobilized over a pH glass electrode. Penicillin is measured indirectly by detecting the reduction in pH associated with the penicillinase-catalyzed hydrolysis of penicillin to penicilloic acid. More recently, this concept has been adapted to FET technology [Caras and Janata 1980] by depositing penicillinase over a pH-sensitive FET. The device consists of two separate gate regions, a penicillin-sensitive gate (coated with the enzyme) and a reference gate that exhibits only pH response. The probe exhibits a number of advantageous features, including:

- minimal effects of temperature and ambient pH variation;
- shelf life of two months;
- requires only a small amount of enzyme; and
- rapid response time (25 sec).

Other enzyme-based FET, similar to the above, could be developed to detect other fermentation products.

Another proposed industrial application is the detection of corrosion in pipes and oil storage tanks [Yanchinski 1982]. In this case, bacteria are imbedded in the membrane surrounding the sensing fluid. Corrosion is often due to bacteria that reduce sulfates to sulfide ions. If these bacteria are incorporated in the sensing mechanism, the FET could detect the sulfide ion potentials released during this reaction. Inserted in the pipe or tank, this device could provide early detection of corrosion with the cost of physical inspection.

Environmental Applications. Environmental monitoring often involves the detection of small quantities of substances in a variety of media. Although advanced analytical systems, such as gas chromatography/mass spectrometry, have improved the sensitivity with which these measurements can be made and have increased the number of substances that can be detected readily, the technology remains costly and difficult to apply to field conditions. The advantages of FET in terms of sensitivity, size, ruggedness and simplicity of operation would seem to apply to environmental sensing as they do for biomedical and industrial applications. In spite of this, an initial survey revealed very little applied R&D focused on environmental uses of FET. Environmental applications can, however, be envisioned as outgrowths of the work in biomedical, military and other areas. For example, a probe with multiple ion or molecular detection capability combined with an integrated circuit chip could be designed to detect and interpret chemical "signatures" of interest (i.e., the groups of compounds identified with particular pollution sources). Other potential environmental applications of biosensor technology include:

- detection of trace amounts of toxic substances in air and water (e.g., detection of volatilized toxins in the air over a hazardous waste site);
- industrial hygiene monitoring (e.g., a potentially more sensitive replacement for the badges worn by workers to detect exposure to hazardous substances); and
- indoor air pollution—the technology might permit manufacture of low-cost sensors for detecting trace air pollutants in home and office environments.

The combination of low cost, small size, ruggedness and capability for multiple detection and signal processing should lead to increased R&D on uses of biological FET in environmental monitoring.

Defense Applications. The U.S. Department of Defense (DOD) has been one of the major sponsors of research in FET sensor development. Dating back to the early 1960s, DOD has sponsored studies on the use of enzyme systems in developing alarm systems for the presence of organophosphate nerve agents. The toxic effect of these agents is based on inhibition of the cholinesterase enzyme. Early work was directed toward development of immobilized enzyme electrodes that could meet the criteria:

- sensitivity of 1 ppb;
- response time of less than 10 sec; and
- high selectivity of response (i.e., no false alarms).

Although enzyme electrodes meeting these criteria were developed [Guilbault 1978], recent attention has turned to the application of chem FET, including an enzyme-coupled device based on the same principle of cholinesterase inhibition (the transistor detects the change of potential caused by changing enzyme activity, which, in turn, is a result of inhibition by the organophosphate compounds). In a recent performance analysis, Janati et al. [1981] found that the advantages of small size, high sensitivity and low cost must be balanced against the disadvantages associated with the irreversibility of the enzyme reaction and the limited usable lifetime (hours rather than days). Although future improvements in shelf life are likely, the irreversible nature of the enzyme inhibition reaction may prove a significant barrier to future widespread use of an enzyme-based FET as a nerve gas detection technology [Janati et al. 1981].

As with civilian areas, the possibilities for defense applications extend to any chemical monitoring situation in which sensitivity, low cost, small size and reliability are useful. In addition to detection of chemical and biological agents under battlefield conditions, biosensors might be used in future verification monitoring of agreements to limit the development and use of such weapons. In this case, the capacity for incorporating signal processing functions with the sensor could facilitate automated monitoring from a single control center, thus limiting the need for onsite verification. Beyond chemical and biological warfare, other defense uses might include submarine detection, taking advantage of the low cost/high sensitivity of FET to surreptitiously monitor wide areas [McAlear 1982a].

The state-of-the-art, therefore, in biosensor technology is well advanced in terms of basic design features and successful prototypes. However, the technology has not yet been commercialized, and the full range of potential applications remains to be explored. The technical barriers to full exploitation of biosensors and the likely direction of future R&D are discussed below.

Future Outlook

Although the trend in R&D is likely to continue to be application-oriented, some general technical barriers will have to be addressed before the technology can be widely commercialized. These barriers, including problems relating to reliability, operating limitations and fabrication, are summarized in Table 7-8. In addition to addressing problems relating to

Table 7-8. Technical Barriers to Biosensor Development [Janati and Huber 1979; Schenck 1978]

Problem Area	Examples	Remarks
Reliability	Ion migration in the gate insulator	Particularly important in ion-selective FET and a function of the manufacturing process and operating conditions (e.g., temperature)
	Degradation of the gate insulator	A problem with both chem and ion-selective FET, often due to hydrolysis of the gate surface
	Contamination	Adsorption of unknown molecules or ions to the insulator surface or the reference electrode can alter the calibration of the sensor
	Current leakage	This problem relates to fabrication methods (discussed below)
Physical Limitations	Reproducibility and hysteresis	The degree of hysteresis that can be tolerated will depend on the application
	Selectivity	A critical requirement for many sensor applications; biological systems are not always selective in response (e.g., more than 100 compounds are known to inhibit cholinesterase in solution)
	Photosensitivity	Gate electrodes may be sensitive to light input
	Debye length effects	If the reaction being sensed is more than the Debye length from the insulator surface, the electrostatic charge is shielded, thus reducing the sensitivity of the device. This poses limitations on the film thickness surrounding the gate and the salt concentration of the solution
Fabrication Technology	Encapsulation	Involves exposing the gate region while sealing all other components from the solution; epoxy resins and silicon rubbers have been used, but these are not readily adapted to mass production; a thick film of silicon nitride has been proposed as an approach compatible with mass production
	Membrane deposition	An automated process is yet to be developed
	Availability of technology	The number of research laboratories (especially universities) with microfabrication capability is limited

Table 7-9. Partial List of Persons and/or Organizations in the United States Involved in Biosensor Development

Organization and/or Individual	Involvement
J. Janati, Department of Bioengineering, University of Utah, Salt Lake City, UT	Research on a variety of applications of FET technology
P. K. Clifford and D. T. Tuma, Department of Electrical Engineering, Carnegie-Mellon University, Pittsburgh, PA	FET devices for gas sensing
International Telephone and Telegraph, New York, NY	Penicillin sensor for use with industrial fermenters
Johnson and Johnson, New Brunswick, NJ	Development of chem FET to measure blood electrolytes
E. S. Kolesar, Jr., Air Force Systems Command, U.S. Air Force School of Medicine, Brooks Air Force Base, TX	Development of chem FET to detect organophosphorus compounds
General Electric Company, Schenectady, NY	Development of FET for detection of biological reactions

the performance and fabrication of sensing devices, research will be required to identify and adequately characterize the biological reactions on which future sensors can be based. A partial list of persons and organizations in the United States conducting biosensor research is given in Table 7-9.

As the above-mentioned problems are resolved, and commercially feasible manufacturing and performance standards are met, research is likely to shift more toward integrating biosensors into the measurement systems required in each application. For example, in many medical applications, the device will be inserted or implanted in the body and will therefore require sterilization and/or appropriate encapsulation. Conventional means of sterilization such as heat or irradiation could not be used, because they would damage the sensor (application of gaseous ethylene oxide is one alternative under investigation) [Janati and Huber 1979]. Catheters with sensors inserted in them are being developed as medical probes [Janati and Huber 1979].

Over the next 5–10 years it is likely that many of the technical barriers will be resolved, leading to the first wide-scale commercial application of biosensors. As the leading developers gain experience, the pattern typical of other areas of microelectronics is likely to be observed: reduced unit cost coupled with improved performance.

CHAPTER 8

THE FUTURE OF BIOELECTRONICS

The future of bioelectronics will be determined by (1) the nature and rate of technical progress, and (2) the market demand for the resultant bioelectronic devices. In Chapter 8, the former is discussed and predictions are ventured regarding the time schedule at which various technical hurdles will be overcome. These time schedules depend, however, on the second of the factors mentioned above—the market demand for bioelectronic devices. Once such devices are advanced to the stage of commercial feasibility, their market penetration will be determined, in large part, by the capacity of industry to incorporate new designs, structures and functions beyond those associated with conventional electronics. Stated another way, the first computer (or other electronic system) incorporating biochips is likely to differ markedly in design and function from the existing state-of-the-art. Below are some observations regarding the technical and economic evolution of the microelectronics industry generally and the role that bioelectronics might play.

INNOVATION IN MICROELECTRONICS

Progress in microelectronics is generally marked by the number of functions that can be packed onto a single device. Hence, stages in the evolution of microelectronics over the 20 years since the introduction of the integrated circuit are identified by the scale of integration:

- small-scale integration (SSI): feature sizes of 25 μm;
- medium-scale integration (MSI): 10-μm features;
- early large-scale integration (LSI): 5-μm features;
- current LSI: 2-μm features; and
- near-future VLSI: 1-μm features.

Over this period of development, various areas of knowledge and skill have been applied to further the state-of-the-art [Mead 1981; Moralee 1982]. The fundamental solid-state physics of semiconductors, which provides the basis for integrated circuit function, is now a mature science. Device fabrication technology has also progressed rapidly to provide the means for constructing chips of increasing complexity. The advents of LSI and VLSI resulted in increased emphasis on a third aspect of microelectronics: circuit and logic design. As mentioned earlier, approaches to device design have changed significantly over the past two decades to the point that hardware design now relies heavily on software techniques, i.e., special rules for circuit layout and design programming languages adapted from conventional software languages. Illustrative of this trend is the term "silicon compiler" used by hardware designers to refer to computer-aided design systems currently under development. Analogous to a conventional software compiler, the silicon compiler will convert linguistic representations of hardware elements to machine code, which can be stored and subsequently used in computer-assisted fabrication.

The evolution of the component fields comprising microelectronics technology is depicted in Figure 8-1. The three well advanced areas in Figure 8-1 are device physics, fabrication and design. In contrast, the equally important areas of large system design and concurrent system architecture are at an early stage of development. The former is evolving out of the computer-aided hardware design systems mentioned above. The latter, concurrent system architecture, has received some limited attention in conventional computer systems in the form of time-sharing and small-scale multiprocessing. However, the prospect of low-cost VLSI technology has opened up the possibility of large-scale multiprocessing (i.e., simultaneous operation). With the increased packing densities offered by VLSI, the opportunity exists to incorporate several complete computer systems (processor, memory and interfaces) onto a single chip. Using conventional architecture (in which processing and memory are represented by distinct units) would not, in this case, result in efficient concurrent operation. What is required, instead, is a fundamentally different structuring of processing and memory functions, perhaps in the direction of merged processor/memory units [Moralee 1981]. Theoretical approaches to this new generation of computer architecture are now being advanced and will undoubtedly be followed by significant departures from conventional concepts in software development as well.

The future of bioelectronics is related to VLSI innovation in two different aspects:

- the similarities shared by the two technologies in terms of designing, fabricating and manipulating extremely complex systems; and

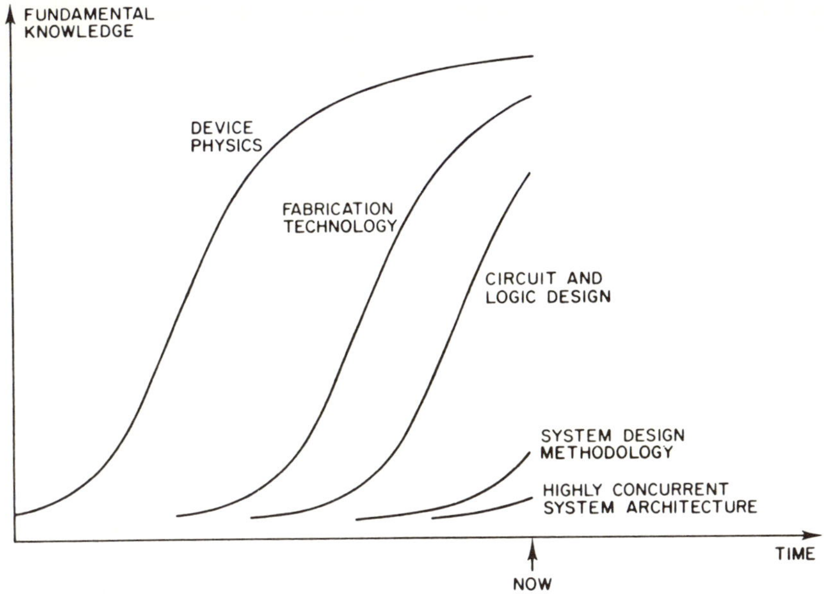

Figure 8-1. Knowledge and skills involved in the evolution of microelectronics [Mean 1981].

- the fundamental differences between the technologies in terms of materials, methods and required skills.

Both the semiconductor/VLSI and biological/chemical approaches to microelectronics, by virtue of their extreme miniaturization, must address the generic issue of complexity. In this respect, work in areas such as advanced system design and architecture should benefit both technologies.

However, semiconductor VLSI and bioelectronic technology differ significantly in terms of the intellectual and economic resources available to them. Although the special skills required for VLSI development may result in some changes in the structure of the semiconductor industry (i.e., a trend toward companies specializing in either design or fabrication rather than both), the necessary investment and technology base can be drawn from an existing, highly successful industry. In contrast, the skills and resources necessary for the development of bioelectronics are too divergent in terms of materials, methods and fundamental science to be drawn from any single industrial base. Those involved in the early stages of biochips technology include organic chemists, biochemists, physicists and electrical engineers and, with a few exceptions, their work is conducted at universities, government research laboratories and small research firms.

The response of the semiconductor industry to biochip research has been, by all accounts, highly cautious and skeptical. With the exception of some IBM research on molecular switching [Aviram and Seiden 1974], no active research programs within the industry have been announced, and at least one researcher has used the term "silicon wall" to describe the resistance of the semiconductor industry to the technology being advanced in biochip research and development (R&D).

STRUCTURE OF THE MICROELECTRONICS INDUSTRY

The above indicates that the microelectronics industry, although viewed as the most innovative and even revolutionary of modern industries, is not going to be a major sponsor or otherwise contribute to early research in bioelectronics. The progress toward commercialization of advancing biochip research is likely to be different from that followed within the microelectronics industry in the past.

The two "new ideas" contributing most significantly to the microelectronics revolution were the transistor and the integrated circuit. If the biochip is to be the next major "new idea" in the industry, its beginnings are likely to be very different. At the time of their inventions, the inventors of both the transistor and the integrated circuit were employed at firms already established in the electronics field. Although originally developed at established electronics firms, these two technologies spawned the rapid growth of small companies financed with venture capital. In the 1960s and 1970s these firms flourished, as it was still feasible for a small group to possess the resources and skills to both design and fabricate devices for commercial use. During this rapid growth phase, entrepreneur/scientists, supported with venture capital, could conduct the research necessary to advance the state-of-the-art while at the same time dominating the commercial market. "Silicon Valley" in northern California abounds with such firms.

As the industry enters the VLSI era, with its emphasis on system complexity and refined fabrication technology, there may be a fundamental change in the role that such small, high-technology firms will play. According to Mead [1981], small firms will no longer be able to afford their own fabrication capability. Rather, these firms are likely to focus on new design methodologies and computer architectures, with fabrication provided as a service by a few firms with state-of-the-art production facilities. The relationship between these fabrication firms and individual chip designers would be analogous to that between publishing houses and authors [Mead 1981].

Bioelectronics, therefore, has emerged at a time when the overwhelming complexity of microelectronics dominates, and industrial response to this problem is likely to differ from historical patterns. It is unlikely, therefore, that biochip development will repeat the cycle of invention by existing industry researchers followed by new, venture capital firms capturing the early commercial market. In all likelihood, the first demonstration of a prototype biochip will be at a university or government research facility, rather than a large electronics firm. The complex task of converting a crude prototype to a sophisticated device that can compete in terms of performance and reliability with the then existing VLSI semiconductor technology will be beyond the means of individual small firms.

SCENARIO FOR BIOELECTRONICS

Although merging of biology and microelectronics offers the potential for a quantum advance in technology, this potential will not be realized without greatly expanded R&D. The resources expended in the early research described in this survey is only a small fraction of that which would be required for a full-scale commercial development effort. The ambitious goals of biochip research and the radical departure from conventional semiconductor materials and methods mean that the investment in R&D will have to be long term.

To sustain such a long-term commitment, researchers will have to demonstrate the feasibility of biolectronics by developing prototype devices in which problems relating to materials, fabrication and performance are solved. The source of much of the early research funding is likely to be the federal government (principally the Department of Defense). A successful prototype device, perhaps within the next 10–20 years, would then attract venture capital and, eventually, the major industry investment necessary to design and fabricate devices for widespread use.

REFERENCES

Albisser, A. M., and B. S. Leibel (1978) "Closed Loop Control of Diabetes," in *Theory, Design, and Biomedical Applications of Solid State Chemical Sensors*, P. W. Cheung, et al., Eds. (West Palm Beach, FL: CRC Press, Inc.), pp. 253-262.

Aviram, A., and P. E. Seiden (1974) "Organic Memory Device," U.S. Patent 3,833,894.

Aviram, A., P. E. Seiden and M. A. Ragner (1981) "Theoretical and Experimental Studies of Hemiquinones and Comments on Their Suitability for Molecular Information Storage Elements," in *Proceedings of the Molecular Electronic Devices Workshop*, F. L. Carter, Ed., ADA105816 (Washington, DC: Naval Research Laboratory), pp. 3-16.

Barrett, T. W. (1981) "Parametric Resonance Produced Switching in Hemoglobin with Visible Light," in *Proceedings of the Molecular Electronic Devices Workshop*, F. L. Carter, Ed., ADA105816, (Washington, DC: Naval Research Laboratory), pp. 274-291.

Bussert, J. (1982) "Are Biochips the New Wave?" *Military Electron. Countermeasures* (June), pp. 27-30.

Caras, S., and J. Janata (1980) "Field Effect Transistor Sensitive to Penicillin," *Anal. Chem.* 52:1935-1937.

Carter, F. L., Ed. (1981a) *Proceedings of the Molecular Electronic Devices Workshop*, ADA105816 (Washington, DC: Naval Research Laboratory).

Carter, F. L. (1981b) "Progress in Concepts of Conformational Switching and Molecular Electronic Devices," NRL-MR-4717, Naval Research Laboratory, Washington, DC, p. 24.

Carter, F. L. (1981c) "Conformational Switching at the Molecular Level," in *Proceedings of the Molecular Electronic Devices Workshop*, F. L. Carter, Ed., ADA105816 (Washington, DC: Naval Research Laboratory), pp. 53-75.

Giaever, I. (1974) "Method and Apparatus for Immunological Detection of Biological Particles," U.S. Patent 3,853,467.

Guilbault, G. G. (1978) "Future of Biomembrane Proges," in *Theory, Design, and Biomedical Applications of Solid State Chemical Sensors*, P. W. Cheung, et al. Eds. (West Palm Beach, FL: CRC Press, Inc.), pp. 253-262.

Hameroff, S. R., and R. C. Watt (1981) "Microtubules: Biological Microprocessors?" in *Proceedings of the Molecular Electronic Devices Workshop*,

F. L. Carter, Ed., ADA105816 (Washington, DC: Naval Research Laboratory), pp. 292-309.

Honig, B. (1981) "Visual Pigments: A New Type of Molecular Switching Device," in *Proceedings of the Molecular Electronic Devices Workshop*, F. L. Carter, Ed., ADA105816 (Washington, DC: Naval Research Laboratory), pp. 178-180.

Huxley, H. E. (1958) "The Contraction of Muscle," *Scientific Am.* (November), p. 66.

Janati, J., and R. J. Huber (1979) "Ion-Sensitive Field Effect Transistors," *Ion-Selective Electrode Rev.* 1:31-79.

Janati, J., R. J. Huber, R. Cohen and E. S. Kolesar, Jr. (1981) "Chemically Sensitive Field-Effect Transistor to Detect Organophosphorous Compounds and Pesticides," *Aviation, Space, Environ. Med.* 52(11):666-671.

McAlear, J. H. (1982a) Meeting at The MITRE Corp., McLean, VA, April 15.

McAlear, J. H. (1982b) Presentation at the Interagency Conference on Biomolecular Electronics, sponsored by the National Science Foundation, Washington, DC, May 26.

McAlear, J. H., and J. M. Wehrung (1978a) "Microsubstrates and Method for Making Micropattern Devices," U.S. Patent 4,103,073.

McAlear, J. H., and J. M. Wehrung (1978b) "Microdevice Substrate and Method for Making Micropattern Devices," U.S. Patent 4,103,064.

McAlear, J. H., and J. M. Wehrung (1981) "Biotechnical Electron Devices," in *Proceedings of the 31st Electronic Components Conference* (Newark, DE: Institution of Electrical and Electronics Engineers).

McAlear, J. H., and J. M. Wehrung (1982) "Towards Three-Dimensional Biomolecular Logic," paper presented at the Interagency Conference on Biomolecular Electronics, sponsored by the National Science Foundation, Washington, DC, May 26.

McAuliffe, K. (1981) "Biochip Revolution," *Omni* (December), pp. 53-58.

Mead, C. A. (1981) "VLSI and Technological Innovation," in *VLSI81: Very Large Scale Integration*, J. P. Gray, Ed. (London: Academic Press, Ltd.), pp. 3-11.

Moralee, D. (1982) "Visions of the VLSI Future," *Electron. Power* (April), pp. 301-305.

Pollack, A. (1982) "Computers from Bacteria," *New York Times* (February 18), p. D2.

Schenck, J. F. (1978) "Technical Difficulties Remaining to the Application of ISFET Devices," in *Theory, Design, and Biomedical Applications of Solid State Chemical Sensors,* P. W. Cheung, et al., Eds. (West Palm Beach, FL: CRC Press, Inc.), pp. 165-173.

Schenck, J. F. (1980) "Field Effect Transistor for Detection of Biological Reactions," U.S. Patent 4,238,757.

Shipman, L. L. (1981) "Two-Electron Gates in Photosynthesis," in *Proceedings of the Molecular Electronic Devices Workshop*, F. L. Carter, Ed., ADA105816 (Washington, DC: Naval Research Laboratory), pp. 46-52.

Ulmer, K. M. (1981) "Biological Assembly of Molecular Ultracircuits," in *Proceedings of the Molecular Electronic Devices Workshop*, F. L. Carter, Ed. ADA105816 (Washington, DC: Naval Research Laboratory), pp. 167-177.

Wohltjen, H. (1981) "Microfabrication Techniques: Current and Future," in *Proceedings of the Molecular Electronic Devices Workshop*, F. L. Carter, Ed., ADA105816 (Naval Research Laboratory).

Yanchinski, S. (1982) "Biochips Speed up Chemical Analysis," *New Scientist* (January 28), p. 236.

INDEX